Feasting with Christ

# FEASTING WITH CHRIST

*Meditations on the Lord's Supper*

Compiled and edited
by
Joel R. Beeke and Paul M. Smalley

PUBLISHING WITH A MISSION

EP BOOKS
Faverdale North, Darlington, DL3 0PH, England

e-mail: sales@epbooks.org

web: http://www.epbooks.org

First published 2012

**British Library Cataloguing in Publication Data available**

ISBN-13: 978-0-85234-794-2     ISBN-10: 0-85234794-4

Unless otherwise indicated, all Scripture quotations are from The Holy Bible, Authorized (King James) Version.

Printed and bound in the USA.

# CONTENTS

# INTRODUCTION

Partaking of the Lord's Supper is one of the Christian's most solemn and sweet acts of worship. Christ commands His disciples: 'This do in remembrance of me' (Luke 22:19). To those who neglect the Supper, Thomas Wadsworth says, 'I beseech you, consider whose command it is you break. It is the command of the Lord Jesus; to remember Him in this Supper is a debt you owe to Him, your Saviour, Lord, and Head; it is a command that bears the superscription of the most supreme authority in heaven or earth' (Wadsworth, 136).

Instituted by a loving Saviour for the good of His people, the Holy Supper holds forth rich spiritual benefits. Paul wrote: 'The cup of blessing which we bless, is it not the communion of the blood of Christ? The bread which we break, is it not the communion of the body of Christ?' (1 Cor. 10:16). Just as the worshippers of false gods have 'fellowship with devils' (1 Cor. 10:20), so also those who feast at the Lord's Table have fellowship with Christ by faith.

Though the bread remains bread and the wine is but wine, the holiness of Christ makes His Supper a sacred event. He chose these elements as His memorial in the church, to represent His incarnation and crucifixion, for us and for our salvation. He is present at the Supper just as He is whenever the church gathers in His name (Matt. 18:20). We do not call the Supper a 'sacrament' because it automatically confers grace, but because it is the sign of our sacred bond with Christ,[1] the new covenant in His blood. More than that, it is a means of grace, by which we commune with the risen Christ and are nourished by the life that is in Him. Thus William Fenner warns: 'We must not rush upon the sacrament. [Something] must be done before we can receive it. "Let a man examine himself, and so let him eat of that bread, and drink of that cup"' (Fenner, 102, citing 1 Cor. 11:28).

None of us are worthy of fellowship with Christ, but the Lord Jesus is worthy of our very best. The twofold call to worship Christ is, 'Serve the LORD with fear, and rejoice with trembling' (Ps. 2:11), and 'Serve the LORD with gladness: come before his presence with singing' (Ps. 100:2). Fear mingles with our gladness; trembling, with our singing. Even beggars may come bowing to the king. The goal is not to become worthy partakers in ourselves, but to partake in a worthy manner. Richard Sibbes writes: 'As we [are accustomed to] say, the king received worthy entertainment in such a gentleman's house, not for that he was worthy to receive him, but because he omitted no compliments and service in his power fit to entertain him' (Sibbes, 4:62).

---

1    From the Latin, *sacramentum*, literally, 'a thing set apart' or 'the thing that sets apart', referring to any word or act that binds or obligates a person, such as the soldier's solemn oath of allegiance to Rome.

We do not make an idol of the bread and wine, as though they were anything more than what they are. But God is present in His ordinances, and we must not fail to honour Him with our deepest reverence and faith. Therefore the Christian regards the call to feast with Christ as an invitation he dare not ignore, but he dare not accept it without due preparation. When he does approach the Supper repenting of sins, trusting in Christ and resolving to live unto Him, he discovers that Christ is eager to sup with him (Rev. 3:19-20). What a privilege and joy to feast with Jesus Christ at His Table, and to be fed by Him, as 'the true meat and drink of life eternal'.[2]

Many pastors and theologians since the Reformation have preached sermons and written books about the Lord's Supper. Their writings have a richly experiential and devotional flavour. We have drawn brief meditations from these sources with the hope that God will bless their words to your soul.

The book is structured in three parts so as to guide the believer through preparing for the Supper, partaking of the Supper, and reflecting on the Supper in a Christ-centred way. Each chapter contains several short selections from classic texts on the Lord's Supper. We have briefly noted the source at the end with full information in the concluding bibliography for those who would like to read more.

Sometimes the selection does not represent a continuous quotation but collected portions; rather than mar this devotional with many ellipsis marks (…) we have chosen to

---

2    Form for the Administration of the Lord's Supper, 'Doctrinal Standards, Liturgy, and Church Order', *The Psalter* (Grand Rapids: Reformation Heritage Books, 1999), 138.

omit them. Interested readers will spot them easily enough by comparing our text with the original sources. As spelling and capitalization varied widely in the old writings, we have conformed them to modern usage. Pronouns referring to God have been capitalized. We have also emended all Scripture citations to conform to the King James Version of the Holy Bible. Archaic words sometimes receive an explanation in brackets, but otherwise we have left the old language intact. Thus the texts were all selected, sometimes abbreviated, occasionally explained, but never paraphrased. This allows the reader to hear the sources in their own voice, and not our interpretations of them.

We wish to thank our loyal and loving wives, Mary Beeke and Dawn Smalley, without whom projects of this nature could never be completed. Thanks, too, to Ann Dykema for her labours in typing up many of these selections.

In this day when the ordinances of public worship are often corrupted, debased, or neglected, may God be pleased to use this book as one tool among many to lead His people into richer, more reverent communion with the living Christ. 'Unto him that loved us, and washed us from our sins in his own blood, and hath made us kings and priests unto God and his Father; to him be glory and dominion for ever and ever. Amen' (Rev. 1:5b-6).

**Joel R. Beeke and Paul M. Smalley**

# NOTE TO THE READER

from the late Rev. Mr John Flavel,
Minister of Darmouth

Examine thyself, reader, whether there be any gracious principle planted in thy soul, whereby thou art alive indeed unto God. Dead souls can have no communion with the living God.

Even a believer himself doth not eat and drink worthily, unless the grace that is in him be excited and exercised at this ordinance.

It is not faith inhering, but faith, realizing, applying and powerfully working. It is not a disposition to humiliation of sins, but the actual thawing and melting of the heart for sin, nor is it a disposition or principle of love to Christ that is only required, but the stirring up of that fire of love, the exciting of it into a vehement flame.

To assist thee in this work, some help is offered in the following meditations. It is true, it is not the reading of the best meditations another can prepare for thee, that will alter the temper of thy heart, except the Spirit of God concur [work together] with these truths, and bless them to thy soul: but yet these helps must not be slighted.

Prepare with all diligence for thy duty. Take pains with thy dull heart; cleanse thy polluted heart; compose thy vain heart; remember how great a presence thou art approaching.

But take ye heed, on the other side, that thou rely not upon thy best preparation. It is an ingenious, and true note of Luther (speaking to this very point of preparation for the sacrament), 'Never are men more unfit, than when they think themselves most fit, and best prepared for their duty; never more fit, than when most humbled and ashamed, in a sense of their own unfitness.'

**Flavel, 6:379–80**

# PART I
# PREPARING BEFOREHAND

# 1

# INFORMING YOUR MIND

*For I have received of the Lord*
*that which also I delivered unto you,*
*that the Lord Jesus the same night*
*in which he was betrayed took bread*
(1 Corinthians 11:23).

## What is the Lord's Supper?

Q What is the Lord's Supper?
A. The Lord's Supper is a sacrament of the New Testament, wherein by giving and receiving bread and wine, according to Christ's appointment, His death is shown forth, and the worthy receivers are, not after a corporal or carnal manner but by faith, made partakers of His body and blood, with all His benefits, to their spiritual nourishment and growth in grace. The end of this is to confirm their union and communion with Christ, renewing their covenant with God,

their thankfulness to Him, and their mutual love for and fellowship one with another as members of the same mystical body (Matt. 26:26-28; 1 Cor. 11:23-26; 10:6-17).

Q. Who is the author of this sacrament?

A. The Lord Jesus Christ, who is the glorious King and Head of His Church, to whom alone it appertains to institute her ordinances.

Q. What may we learn from its being Christ's ordinance?

A. That we ought therefore to have a special regard for it, and beware of either neglecting or abusing it.

Q. What are the usual names and designations given to this ordinance?

A. It is called the sacrament of the Lord's Supper, the Lord's Table, the communion, the breaking of the bread, the cup of blessing, Christ's testament, the feast, and the Eucharist (1 Cor. 11:20; 10:16; 5:8; Acts 2:46; Luke 22:20).

Q. Why is it called the sacrament?

A. It is called so by way of distinction, and because here we take a most solemn oath of fidelity to our Redeemer.

Q. Why is it called the Lord's Supper?

A. Because:

1. It was instituted when Christ was eating the Passover supper with His disciples, which was at night.

2. The supper then was accounted the principal meal of the family.

3. It is ordained only for those who dwell in Christ's family and abide with Him both day and night.

Q. Why is it called the Lord's Table?

A. Because He is the author of it; yea, He is both the maker and the matter of this entertainment, the feeder and the food also.

Q. Why is it called the communion?

A. Because, in the right partaking of this ordinance, we have communion and fellowship with Christ, share with Him in the benefits of His death and purchase, and also have communion one with another.

Q. Why is it called the breaking of bread?

A. Because, in this ordinance, bread is broken and made use of, as the outward symbol and seal of Christ's wounded and broken body, with all the glorious benefits flowing therefrom.

Q. Why is it called the cup of blessing?

A. Because:

1. In using it, we bless God for His free love toward us in Christ.

2. It contains, offers, and seals to us, in a sacramental way, all the blessings of the new covenant.

Q. Why is it called Christ's testament?

A. Because in this ordinance we have Christ's testament and last will sealed, and a copy of it put into the believer's hand, containing the rich legacies He has left them.

Q. Why is it called a feast?

A. Because hereby the believers are richly entertained by Christ, having sweet intimacy with Him and great expressions of His love. And their souls are nourished and strengthened for duty. It is both a marriage feast and a feast of commemoration.

Q. Why is it called the Eucharist by the ancients?

A. It signifies thanksgiving because:

1. When this sacrament was instituted, it both began and ended with the giving of thanks.

2. Because the great design of it is to keep up the thankful remembrance of Christ's death and redeeming love. And when believers partake, they should, with their whole souls, give thanks to God because He is good, and sing, 'Glory to God in the highest.'

**Willison, *Sacramental Catechism*, 68, 71–73**

### Spiritual food for the spiritually alive

The first matter to be considered is the *Author* of this sacrament of the Lord's Supper; He is the Lord Jesus Christ (*cf.* the historical record in Matt. 26; Mark 14; and Luke 22). The apostle repeats this institution in 1 Corinthians 11:23-27.

The second matter to be considered in reference to this sacrament is the *external signs*. We must here take note of the signs and the ceremonies associated with them. The signs are identical to those used in meals in order to nourish and refresh the body: *bread and wine*. Christ broke the bread, thereby signifying the breaking of His body, that is, His death.

Thirdly, we must reflect upon the *matter signified* in the Lord's Supper. The signs have not been instituted for the purpose of serving God by partaking of them, for God is a Spirit who must be served in a spiritual manner. Christ is this food and drink. By way of natural food and drink, that is, bread and wine, the Lord signifies the spiritual: Christ's body and blood. When seeing these signs, the communicant must not end in them mentally, but must proceed to the matter signified, that is, to the body and blood of Christ broken and shed to satisfy God's justice for the sins of believers.

The fourth matter to be considered is the harmony between the sign and the matter signified, this being nourishment and refreshment. Thus as bread and wine have a nourishing and invigorating power when one partakes of them, Christ's body and blood (His suffering and death) upon being received by faith likewise nourish, strengthen, and invigorate spiritual life.

**Brakel, 525–529, 532**

### The humble Saviour offered to the poor

The elements or matter, of which it consisteth, [are] consecrated bread and wine. It neither stood with the outward poverty of Christ, nor with the benefit of the church, to institute such sumptuous and gaudy elements, as might possess too much the sense of the beholder, and too little resemble the quality of the Saviour. And therefore He chose His sacraments rather for the fitness, than the beauty of them; as respecting more the end, than the splendour or riches, of His Table; and intended rather to manifest His divine power in altering poor elements into a precious use, than to exhibit any carnal pomp, in such delicious fare, as did not agree with the spiritualness of His kingdom.

Though He be contented, out of tenderness toward our weakness, to stoop unto our senses, yet he will not cocker [indulge] them: as in His real and natural body, so in His representative, the sacrament, — a sensual or carnal eye sees not either form or beauty (Isa. 53:2), for which it may be desired. Pictures ought to resemble their originals; and the sacrament, we know, is the picture or type of Him who was a man of sorrow (Isa. 53:3); and this picture was drawn, when the day of God's fierce wrath was upon Him (Lam. 1:12): and can we expect from it any satisfaction or pleasure to the senses? This body was naked on the cross; it were incongruous to have the sacrament of it pompous on the Table. As it was the will of the Father, which Christ both glorifies and admires, to reveal unto babes what he hath hidden from the wise; so is it here his wisdom to communicate, by the meanest [simplest] instruments, what he hath denied unto the choicest delicates, to feed His Daniels rather with pulse [vegetables], than with all the dainties on the king's table.

And if we observe it, divine miracles take ever the poorest and meanest subject to manifest themselves on. If He want an army to protect His church, flies (Isa. 7:18), and frogs, and caterpillars (Ex. 8:6, 24), and lamps, and pitchers (Judg. 7:20; Josh. 6:4; Judg. 15:15), etc. shall be the strongest soldiers (Joel 2:25) and weapons He useth; the lame and the blind (John 5:23; Matt 12:10), the dumb (John 9:1), and the dead (Matt. 9:25), water (Matt. 12:22), and clay (John 2:7), these are

materials for His power (John 9:6). — Even where thou seest
the instruments of God weakest, there expect and admire the
more abundant manifestation of His greatness and wisdom:
undervalue not the bread and wine in this holy Sacrament,
which do better resemble the benefits of Christ crucified,
than any other the choicest delicates.

**Reynolds, 24–25**

## A sacred obligation for all Christians

[It obligates] every Christian of age and understanding to
come to the Lord's Supper, or to provide themselves, with
such an excuse as they think will satisfy Christ the Judge,
when He shall ask them at the Last Day, why they did not
comply with that command of His, the night before He died,
to 'Do this in remembrance of Him'?

For, this command of Christ being given to none but the
apostles in person, will either oblige none else, or necessarily
take in all Christians of age and understanding: and that the
apostles understood it to oblige all other Christians, as well as
themselves, appears from the practice immediately following
(which is always the best expounder of a law), which was, that
the apostles and other Christians met together in religious
assemblies, and partook alike of the Lord's Supper.

And that this was the custom of the churches, where the
apostles were not present, appears from the history of the
Corinthians abusing this sacrament (1 Cor. 11), as also from
the argument with St Paul, from the Christians communicating
in bread and wine (1 Cor. 10) in order to deter them from

eating things offered to idols. Now this communicating being made, by St Paul, in that argument, a badge of their belonging to Christ, as the eating things offered to idols was the token of an idolater, it is plain he supposes all Christians obliged, at time and place convenient, to communicate. And if it had not been, in his time, the custom for Christians to come to the Lord's Table, his argument had had no force at all in the tenth chapter. And if it had not been their duty to come to the sacrament, he would not in the eleventh chapter have reproved them for coming in so irreverent and disorderly a manner, but have forbidden their coming at all; for why should they commemorate Christ's death unworthily, and to their great peril, since there was no obligation on them to commemorate it at all? Since therefore he bids them examine themselves, and come, he knows it is absolutely necessary that they should come; and this necessity could only arise from Christ's command given to the apostles at His Last Supper, and repeated to St Paul himself by Christ.

From all which you may see that all Christians are certainly obliged to come to the Lord's Table; and that no one should exempt himself from obeying this command, whom Christ hath not exempted. Let them therefore look well to it, who seldom or never partake of the Lord's Supper.

**Fleetwood, 7–9**

### A remarkable help to believers

[T]he believing and affectionate remembrance of Christ [in the Lord's Supper] is of singular advantage at all times to the people of God. For it is the immediate end of one of the greatest ordinances that ever Christ appointed to the church.

To have frequent recognitions of Christ, will appear to be singularly efficacious [productive] and useful to believers, if you consider,

1. If at any time the heart be dead and hard, this is the likeliest means in the world to dissolve, melt, and quicken it. Look hither, hard heart; hard indeed if this hammer will not break it. Behold the blood of Jesus.

2. Art thou easily overcome by temptations to sin? This is the most powerful restraint in the world from sin: Romans 6:2, 'How shall we, that are dead to sin, live any longer therein?' We are crucified with Christ, what have we to do with sin? Have such a thought as this, when thy heart is yielding to temptation. How can I do this, and crucify the Son of God afresh! Hath He not suffered enough already on earth; shall I yet make Him groan as it were for me in heaven! Look, as David poured the water brought from the well of Bethlehem, on the ground, though he was athirst, for he said, it is the blood of the men. That is, they eminently hazarded their lives to fetch it; much more should a Christian pour out upon the ground, yea, despise and trample under foot, the greatest profit or pleasure of sin; saying, Nay, I will have nothing to do with it, I will on no terms touch it, for it is the blood of Christ: it cost blood, infinite, precious blood to expiate it. If there were a knife in your house that had been thrust to the heart of your father, you would not take pleasure to see that knife, much less to use it.

3.  Are you afraid your sins are not pardoned, but still stand upon account before the Lord? What more relieving, what more satisfying, than to see the cup of the New Testament in the blood of Christ, which is 'shed for many for the remission of sins'? Who shall lay anything to the charge of God's elect? It is 'Christ that died'.

4.  Are you staggered at your sufferings, and hard things you must endure for Christ in this world? Doth the flesh shrink back from these things, and cry, spare thyself? What is there in the world more likely to steel and fortify thy spirit with resolution and courage, than such a sight as this? Did Christ face the wrath of men, and the wrath of God too? Did He stand as a pillar of brass, with unbroken patience, and stedfast resolution, under such troubles as never met in the like height upon any mere creature, till death beat the last breath out of His nostrils? And shall I shrink for a trifle? Ah, He did not serve me so! I will arm myself with the like mind (1 Peter 2:21).

5.  Is thy faith staggered at the promises? Canst thou not rest upon a promise? Here is what will help thee against hope to believe in hope, giving glory to God. For this is God's seal added to His covenant, which ratifies and binds fast all that God hath spoken.

6. Dost thou idle away precious time vainly, and live unusefully to Christ in thy generation? What more apt both to convince and cure thee, than such remembrance of Christ as this? O when thou considerest thou art not thine own, thy

time, thy talents are not thine own, but Christ's; when thou shalt see thou art bought with a price (a great price indeed) and so art strictly obliged to glorify God, with thy soul and body, which are His (2 Cor. 5:14), this will powerfully awaken a dull, sluggish, and lazy spirit. In a word, what grace is there that this remembrance of Christ cannot quicken? What sin cannot it mortify? What duty cannot it animate? O it is of singular use in all cases to the people of God.

**Flavel, 1:269–70**

## 2

# FOCUSING YOUR FAITH

*Christ our passover is sacrificed for us*
(1 Corinthians 5:7b).

## The great love of Christ for sinners

Was ever love indeed like His? Well may it be called love which passeth knowledge. Angels are lost in wonder, whilst they look into the mystery of redeeming love; and how then should we, to whom this love is shown, be astonished whilst we are called to partake of it? He died not for angels, but for men; and when? Was it when we were faithful, affectionate and obedient, that we gained His heart to such an expensive manifestation of His love? No; — when we were enemies by wicked works, when we were without strength or power to love or obey Him, even then in due time did Christ die for the ungodly: in us there was nothing but misery, we were lost in sin, willfully lost by our disobedience, without power or inclination to seek for any favor at God's hands; and He wanted not our services, His glory would have been unsullied, if He had given us up to the fruit of our folly, and left us to our deserved ruin; neither can He receive any addition to His happiness by us, who is in Himself all-sufficient, and in His nature infinitely happy, exalted above all blessing and praise.

But, freely moved by the mere benignity [goodness] of His heart, and out of pure compassion to us, Jesus offered to stand in our stead; and since to save us He must be made man, His love stooped to every meanness [poverty or lowliness] of our condition, to the form of a servant, to the death of a slave. Love brought Him down from the throne of glory, love clothed Him with a body like our own, love urged Him on through all the painful steps of His afflicted life; the waters of trouble were never able to quench it, nor the floods of persecution drown it. Love put the cup of trembling into His hand, love bid Him drink the last drop of all its dregs; for having loved his own, He loved them unto the end; His love abode till He cried, 'It is finished'; when, having sealed with blood the sure and well-ordered covenant, His soul was dismissed, and He went to begin His triumphs over death, hell and the grave; and when He arose again, love was His first expression, 'Go to my brethren, and say, I ascend to my Father and your Father.' Love carried Him to the right hand of God, and there He is this moment showing forth the unchangeableness of His affection, by ever living to make intercession for us, and pleading before the throne the marks of love so deeply engraven in His hands and in His side. And when can we then be called so feelingly to remember this love, as at an ordinance where all its glory is made to pass before us?

**Haweis, 13–15**

## Christ made sin, we made righteous

'For he hath made him to be sin for us, who knew no sin; that we might be made the righteousness of God in him' (2 Cor. 5:21). There are three things concerning God the Father, three things concerning the Son, and three things concerning ourselves, all in these words that I have mentioned, and all suitable for us to be acting faith upon.

I.  I would remember, if the Lord help me, the sovereignty of God the Father, His justice, and His grace.

1. *The sovereignty of God*. I could mention that this sovereignty of God extends itself to all persons chosen, and show for whom Christ should be made sin; for He was not made sin for all, but for them who became 'the righteousness of God in him': also the sovereignty of God over things, dispensing with the law so far, that He suffered for sin 'who knew no sin'; and we, who had sinned, were let go free; — the sovereignty of God in appointing the Son to this work, 'He made him'; for none else could — He was the servant of the Father. So that the whole foundation of this great transaction lies in the sovereignty of God over persons and things, in reference to Christ. Let us, then, remember to bow down to the sovereignty of God in this ordinance of the Lord's Supper.

2. *There is the justice of God*. 'He made him to be sin' — imputed sin unto Him, reckoned unto Him all the sins of the elect, caused all our sins to meet upon Him, made Him a sin-offering, a sacrifice for sin, laid all the punishment of

our sins upon Him. To this end He sent Him forth to be a propitiation for sin, to declare His righteousness. The Lord help us to remember that His righteousness is in a special manner exalted by the death of Christ. He would not save us any other way but by making Him sin.

3. *There is the grace of God*, [which] manifests itself in the aim and design of God in all this matter. What did God aim at? It was 'that we might become the righteousness of God in him' — that we might be made righteous, and freed from sin.

II. There are three things that lie clear in the words, that we may call to remembrance, concerning the Son.

1. There are many things in Scripture that direct us to thoughts of *the spotless purity, righteousness, and holiness of Christ*, when we think of His sufferings. A 'Lamb of God, without spot'. He 'did no sin, nor had any guile in his mouth'. He was 'holy, harmless, undefiled, separate from sinners'. Faith should call this to mind in the sufferings of Christ, that He 'knew no sin'. That expression sets sin at the greatest distance from Jesus Christ.

2. *The sufferings of Christ*. 'He was made sin' — a comprehensive word, that sets out His whole sufferings. Look, whatever the justice of God, the law of God, whatever the threatenings of God did require to be inflicted as a punishment for sin, Christ underwent it all. [W]e see not the thousandth part of the evil of sin, that follows inseparably from the righteousness and holiness of God yet, whatever it was, Christ underwent it all.

3. Then there is *the merit of Christ*; which is another object of faith that we should call over in the celebration of this ordinance. Why was 'he made sin'? It was 'that we might become the righteousness of God in him'. It is answerable to that other expression in Galatians 3:13-14, He hath borne the curse — was 'made a curse for us'. To what end? That 'the blessing of Abraham might come upon us'; or, that we might be completely made righteous. The design of our assembling together, is to remember how we come to be made righteous. It is, by Christ's being made sin.

III. We may see three things concerning ourselves:

1. *Our own sin and guilt*: He was made sin 'for us'. If Christ was made sin for us, then we were sinners.

2. We may remember *our deliverance* — how we were delivered from sin, and all the evils of it. It was not by a word of command or power, or by the interposition of saints or angels, or by our own endeavours; but by the sufferings of the Son of God. And,

3. God would have us remember and call to mind the state whereinto we are brought — which is *a state of righteousness*; that we may bless Him for that which in this world will issue in our righteousness, and in the world to come, eternal glory. These things we may call over for our faith to meditate upon. Our minds are apt to be distracted; the ordinance is to fix them: and if we act faith in an especial manner in this ordinance, God will be glorified.

**Owen, 521–23**

## The justice of God satisfied

Herein remember also the inexorable justice of God. Though love would pardon, yet must it be in a way wherein justice should be satisfied. Sin required an expiation equivalent to its high demerit; neither earth nor heaven afforded any such; I looked, and there was none to help. Justice demanded righteous judgement, such as had been poured upon rebel angels cast down into hell on their first transgression; the thunderbolt of wrath was lifted up to smite us sinners to the lowest pit. Jesus steps between, and cries, Stay them from going down to the pit, I have found a ransom; receives the deadly shafts in His own body on the tree, and manifests the justice of God more gloriously than could have been done by the destruction of the whole human race. For who is this? This is Jesus the Son of God, the brightness of His glory, the express image of His person; this is the Father's equal, the man that is His fellow; this is the eternal God, come to expiate His creatures' crimes. Satisfaction was demanded; He offers to pay, to over-pay every demand.

The price agreed, the Judge executes His claim. Awake my sword, He cries, against the Shepherd; the sword awoke to smite to the uttermost, and take full vengeance for the sins of a fallen world. It pleased the Lord to put Him to grief; He laid upon Him the iniquities of us all; and what would have utterly crushed us into hell, bruised to death the only Son of God. Behold the severity of God; He spared not His own Son; see herein what a flaming sword justice holds, and how it is honored by such a sacrifice; see from hence what a fearful thing it is to fall into the hands of the living God; and in this ordinance learn to tremble whilst you see nothing but the blood of God Himself capable of expiating your guilt, and satisfying the demands of His own inexorable Law.

**Haweis, 17–18**

## Setting our eyes on the precious blood

A believer should eye the blood of Christ in the Lord's Supper in the several properties, virtue, and efficacy of it till suitable graces thereby are drawn forth into action.

Eye the blood of Christ in the sacrament, as it is a *precious* blood. 1 Peter 1:18-19: We 'were not redeemed with corruptible things, as silver and gold … but with the precious blood of Christ'. The dignity and excellency of Christ's person make it so exceedingly precious, being the blood of that person who was God as well as man (Acts 20:28).

Eye the blood of Christ in the sacrament, as it is *satisfying* blood. The law of God was transgressed; the covenant of works was violated by us; the justice of God was wronged; and the sinner was indebted unto justice. Eye Christ's blood as the payment of our debt; as shed for our good and in our stead. Christ has endured as much as our sins had deserved. 1 Timothy 2:6: 'Who gave Himself a ransom for all'.

Eye the blood of Christ in the sacrament as *pacifying and reconciling* blood. When sin was expiated, God was appeased. Romans 3:25: 'Whom God hath set forth to be a propitiation through faith in His blood.' 1 John 2:2: 'He is the propitiation for our sins.' By this blood, God's wrath is turned aside.

Eye the blood of Christ in the sacrament as *purchasing* blood. By this He purchased His church and people. Acts 20:28: 'Feed the church of God, which He hath purchased with His own blood.' 1 Corinthians 6:20: 'For ye are bought with a price.'

Eye the blood of Christ in the sacrament as *justifying* blood, as that which makes you righteous in the sight of God, though you have no righteousness of your own. Romans 5:9: 'Much more then, being now justified by His blood, we shall be saved from wrath through Him.'

Eye the blood of Christ in the sacrament as *pardoning* blood, as that by which you have the full, free and everlasting pardon of all your sins. Through this blood of Christ we have redemption, that is, the forgiveness of sins (Eph. 1:7; Col. 1:14).

Eye the blood of Christ in the sacrament as *heart-purifying* blood. Revelation 1:5: 'Who loved us, and washed us from our sins in His own blood'. It was not only holy blood, but it is sanctifying blood.

Eye the blood of Christ in the sacrament as *pleading* blood. Hebrews 12:24: 'The blood of sprinkling, that speaketh better things than that of Abel.' Abel's blood cried for vengeance, but the blood of Christ cries for mercy.

Eye the blood of Christ in the sacrament as *comforting* blood; that it must be because of all the former properties already mentioned. The soul that is scorched with the fiery apprehensions of God's burning displeasure may be cooled by one drop of the blood of Christ. The wounds of your conscience and the wounds of Christ, brought together, will make wholeness.

Eye the blood of Christ in the sacrament as *heart-softening* blood, as that which can dissolve the most stony heart, as that which can break the hardest sinner. Zechariah 12:10: 'They shall look upon Me whom they have pierced, and they shall mourn for Him.'

Eye the blood of Christ in the sacrament as *sin-mortifying* blood. It saves your soul because it kills your sin. This blood will kill your pride, mortify your earthly-mindedness, and subdue all your inordinate affections. Romans 6:6: 'Knowing this, that our old man is crucified with Him, that the body of sin might be destroyed, that henceforth we should not serve sin.'

Eye the blood of Christ in the sacrament as *quickening* blood. It lays your sin sprawling within you and dying in your hearts, but it will give life unto your heart. John 6:53: 'Except ye eat the flesh of the Son of Man, and drink His blood, ye have no life in you.' The blood of Christ is the life of all your graces.

**Doolittle, 80–87**

## Trusting the compassionate healer

'Then came she and worshipped him, saying, Lord, help me' (Matt. 15:25).

Let me take this woman of Canaan as my example in believing. And oh, that my faith may be as strong as hers!

1. *She comes to the Savior* — not to physicians, but to Jesus; for she feels that He alone can do for her what she wants. And is not Christ my Savior, my only Savior? Who else can heal me, can wash out my guilt, and give me peace? He is the great helper of my soul, to whom I must have recourse.

2. *She deeply feels her need.* Had she not, she would not have come to our Lord. She had a poor suffering daughter, for whom she was greatly distressed, and it was a deep sense of her utter need that led her to think of the Savior. Oh, that I felt my wants more deeply! Oh, that my spiritual disease gave me more uneasiness! Then should I feel a more earnest desire for Him, who is the great and good Physician of souls. The more the Holy Spirit convinces me of sin, the more eagerly shall I long for that pardon which Christ alone can give me.

3. *She makes a direct application to Jesus.* She is not content with hearing that He gave relief to this or that sufferer. She wants Him to relieve her. She brings her own case before Him. And shall I be satisfied with the bare belief that He is a Savior — that He hath saved others? No, I must go to Him myself. It is true, I cannot see Him as she did, but I can look to Him with the eye of faith; I can approach Him with a believing heart.

4. *Mark her perseverance.* Jesus at first made as though He regarded her not. But her faith upheld her. She pressed her

cause. She would receive no denial. Here is true faith, the faith that grasps salvation. Christ is at this moment holding out to me all the blessings of His atonement: faith is the hand which I must put forth to receive them. Christ has purchased salvation for me: faith lays hold of it, and makes it mine.

5. *She is accepted.* 'Then Jesus answered and said unto her, O woman, great is thy faith: be it unto thee even as thou wilt.' What an encouragement to me! For is there not acceptance for me also? My faith, alas, is small, but He graciously accepts it. My heart is sadly cold, but He can warm it. I am utterly powerless in myself, but He has said, 'My grace is sufficient for thee, for my strength is made perfect in weakness.'

**Oxenden, 21–22**

# 3

## EXAMINING YOUR LIFE

*Wherefore whosoever shall eat this bread, and drink this cup of the Lord, unworthily, shall be guilty of the body and blood of the Lord. But let a man examine himself, and so let him eat of that bread, and drink of that cup. For he that eateth and drinketh unworthily, eateth and drinketh damnation to himself, not discerning the Lord's body. For this cause many are weak and sickly among you, and many sleep. For if we would judge ourselves, we should not be judged*
(1 Corinthians 11:27-31).

### Receiving the Supper rightly

Question 97: What is required to the worthy receiving of the Lord's Supper?

A. It is required of them that would worthily partake of the Lord's Supper, that they examine themselves of their knowledge to discern the Lord's body; of their faith to feed upon him; of their repentance, love, and new obedience;

lest coming unworthily, they eat and drink judgment to themselves [*Westminster Shorter Catechism*].

Q. 1. What are the duties of worthy receivers?

A. There are three sorts of duties incumbent on them; some antecedent to it, some concomitant of it, and some subsequent to it.

Q. 2. What are the antecedent duties to it?

A. They are two: (1) Examination of their graces; (2) Preparation of their souls.

*Examination of their graces*: 1 Corinthians 11:28-29: 'But let a man examine himself, and so let him eat of that bread, and drink of that cup. For he that eateth and drinketh unworthily, eateth and drinketh damnation to himself, not discerning the Lord's body.'

*Preparation of their souls*: 1 Corinthians 5:8: 'Therefore let us keep the feast, not with old leaven, neither with the leaven of malice and wickedness; but with the unleavened bread of sincerity and truth.'

Q. 3. What is the first grace to be tried?

A. Our saving knowledge of God in Christ, without which we cannot discern the Lord's body.

Q. 4. What are we to enquire of, touching our knowledge of God in Christ?

A. We are to examine whether it be competent for quantity, and savingly operative and influential on the heart and life (Hos. 4:6; 1 Cor. 13:1).

Q. 5. When is knowledge competent and influential?

A. When we truly understand, by the teachings of the Father, the sin and misery of the fall, the nature and necessity of Christ, and under these convictions, come to Him in the way of faith (John 6:45). And subject ourselves to Him in sincere obedience (Matt. 11:28-29).

Q. 6. What are we to examine ourselves about, besides knowledge?

A. We are obliged to examine ourselves about our faith, whether we have it in any saving degree (2 Cor. 13:5). For without faith we cannot please God (Heb. 11:6). Nor enjoy spiritual communion with Christ (Eph. 3:17).

Q. 7. What other grace must be examined and sought for?

A. We must examine our love to Christ, and all that are His: because no gifts signify anything without love (1 Cor. 13:2).

Q. 8. What else must worthy receivers examine themselves about?

A. The sincerity of their hearts, evidenced by their obedience; without which they cannot worthily approach the Table (1 Cor. 5:8).

Q. 9. But if, upon examination we are in doubts about our faith and sincerity, must we forbear?

A. If our doubts arise from the weakness, and not the total want [lack] of grace, such doubts should not hinder us; Romans 14:1: 'Him that is weak in the faith, receive ye.'

Q. 10. What is the danger of coming to the Lord's Table without these graces?

A. The danger is exceeding great both to soul and body (1 Cor. 11:29-30).

**Flavel, 6:289–90**

## Mere knowledge is not enough

Consider, O my soul, that mere knowledge is not a sufficient qualification for the holy communion. If I have knowledge to discern the Lord's body, and want [lack] faith to feed upon Him; I shall return from His Table, disappointed and ashamed.

Do I believe in an unseen Jesus? Do I heartily approve the method which God has appointed for man's salvation, that being justified by faith, he should have peace with God through our Lord Jesus Christ? Do I heartily submit to the righteousness of God? And rejoice in God through Him, by whom we have now received the atonement? Do I earnestly desire to be found in Christ, not having mine own righteousness, but that which is through the faith of Christ, the righteousness which is of God by faith, that Christ may be made unto me righteousness?

I must also inquire concerning my repentance. An impenitent communicant I know must be an unworthy one. That I am a sinner, is a matter past question; and that as such I am exposed to the displeasure of God.

Have I laid these things to heart? Have my convictions been affecting? Have I not only known, but felt these things? Have I been weary and heavy laden under a sense of sin? Yea, have I been ashamed of sin, as a nauseous, loathsome, filthy thing; contrary to the nature and law of God, and my own happiness too, which consists in conformity to God and enjoyment of Him?

Have I been influenced by these convictions to take up a hearty and sincere resolution of better obedience? Do I hate every false way? And have I a respect to all God's commandments? Oh! Let me remember, that nothing is repentance that consists with an habitual love to any sin, or an allowed aversion to any instance of duty, or branch of holiness.

**Earle, 21–24**

## Heart, mouth, and hand

Now then this point comes in, that you have to prove yourselves whether you be in the faith or not; as the apostle says, 'Examine yourselves, whether ye be in the faith' (2 Cor. 13:5). Examine if your soul be seasoned with this faith, for if you have not faith in Christ, Christ is not in you; and if Christ be not in you, you are in an evil state, you are in the estate of the reprobate and the condemned. So every one ought to look carefully and see if he has a belief in the blood of Christ or not: whether or not, he believes to get mercy by His merits and sanctification by His blood. For if thou have no measure of this faith, thou hast no measure of peace with God, for our peace with God is engendered and grows daily more and more by true faith in Christ.

Now this faith where it is true, where it is lively and couples the heart with God, as I have already said, it must break forth in word and deed, it can by no means be held in, but it will break forth. It must break out in word, in glorifying the God of heaven, who has forgiven us our sins; it must break forth in word, by giving a notable confession of those sins wherein we have offended Him. It must break out in deed, in doing good works, to testify to the world that thing which is within thy heart; to testify to the world that thou who hast this faith art a new man; that by thy good example of life and conversation thou mayest edify thy brethren, the simple ones of the church of God; and that by thy holy life thou mayest draw sinners to repentance, that they, seeing thy light, may be compelled to glorify God in thee.

Therefore, in the first point of trial let us look to these three, to the heart, to the mouth, and to the hand.

**Bruce, 156–58**

## Communion with Christ requires communion with Christians

Love to Christians is another branch of that love which is requisite as a previous qualification, fitting persons for worthy receiving of the Lord's Supper, and to that end to be examined before we come.

He that truly loves not his brother, that truly loves not a Christian, is a mere carnal man. For he is in his natural darkness; and walks therein. He is spiritually dead, and in God's account a murderer of his brother; for there is hand-

murder by shedding men's blood; tongue-murder by cruel reproaches, etc.; heart-murder by causeless anger and hatred.

'He that saith he is in the light, and hateth his brother, is in darkness even until now. He that loveth his brother abideth in the light, and there is none occasion of stumbling in him. But he that hateth his brother is in darkness, and walketh in darkness, and knoweth not whither he goeth, because that darkness hath blinded his eyes' (1 John 2:9-11).

And again, it is said: 'He that loveth not his brother abideth in death. Whosoever hateth his brother is a murderer: and ye know that no murderer hath eternal life abiding in him' (1 John 3:14-15). Now he that is a mere carnal man, in his carnal darkness, spiritually dead in sin, a murderer without eternal life abiding in him cannot possibly perform any true service unto God.

The Lord's Supper is a sacramental seal and token, not only of our communion with Christ, but also of our communion with His members, of our fellowship with the saints. This the Apostle clearly intimates, saying, 'For we being many are one bread, and one body: for we are all partakers of that one bread' (1 Cor. 10:17).

**Roberts, 165–67**

## Perfection not required

Persons ought to examine themselves of their fitness before they presume to partake of the Lord's Supper lest, by their unworthy partaking, they eat and drink damnation to themselves.

The fitness or unfitness here spoken of is not that of desert or undeserving; there is no man on earth who deserves such a blessing and privilege. If God had dealt with us according to our deservings, He never would have appointed us any means of grace at all. He never would have appointed such a signification and seal of His infinite mercy and grace. There are in this ordinance the exhibition of the dying love of Christ and the offer made of the benefits of it. Now we are all far from being worthy of such an offer.

Not every unfitness renders the attendance a defective and sinful act in that manner. A man's having so much sin in his heart that he can do no other than attend the Lord's Supper in a very defective manner is not the unfitness we speak of. In this sense all men are also unworthy of any gospel privilege and are unfit for attendance on any gospel duty.

But 'tis such an unfitness as renders the ordinance void. [T]here are some qualifications that make a man so unfit that there is no encouragement in the Word of God of any benefit to such an attendant; it is utterly against the mind and will of God that such should come bringing these unfitnesses with them.

Therefore, before a man comes to this ordinance, he ought to examine himself with respect to these things:

1. Whether or not he lives in any known sin. Those persons who live immoral lives, whatever immorality it is that is their practice, who live in the customary indulgence of any lust

whatsoever, are utterly unfit to come to the holy ordinance of the Lord.

2.  Persons ought to examine whether or not it is their serious resolution to avoid all sin and live in obedience to all known commands as long as he lives.

3. But persons should particularly examine themselves before they come to the Lord's Supper whether or not they don't entertain a spirit of hatred or envy or revenge towards their neighbor. 1 Corinthians 5:8: 'Therefore let us keep the feast, not with old leaven, neither with the leaven of malice and wickedness.'

Persons therefore should particularly examine themselves whether or not they have forgiven their enemies and those who have done them any hurt so as to allow no wishing of any hurt to them. If men have quarrels one with another they should see to it to put an end to 'em before they come to the Lord's Supper.

4.  Persons ought to examine themselves what it is they aim at in coming to the Lord's Supper. The ordinance was appointed for the spiritual good of the partakers. If those therefore who come don't seek that in it, and 'tis not any desire of their spiritual good or from any conscientious regard to God's command that they come, but only for some by-end, some temporal advantage or credit, they eat and drink unworthily.

**Edwards, 100–105**

## 4

## PREPARING YOUR HEART

*Therefore let us keep the feast, not with old leaven, neither with the leaven of malice and wickedness; but with the unleavened bread of sincerity and truth*
(1 Corinthians 5:8).

### Humbled to meet our God

The eternal Son of God, when taking His leave of an ungrateful world, instituted the sacrament of the Supper, as a lively resemblance and memorial of His bloody sufferings and death in the room of His people; and also to be a bright and lasting evidence of the amazing love of God the Father, the Son, and Holy Ghost to perishing sinners.

In this most august ordinance of the New Testament, the great God approaches very near to us, and we to Him; and yet it is to be deeply regretted that many who profess to believe this come to it with so little thought and preparation, and with so much indifference and carelessness of spirit. Oh, shall we adventure so near the great God, who is infinitely holy, in whose sight the heavens are not pure, and in whose presence the sun and stars are dimmed, and the brightest seraphims do gather in their wings, and account themselves as little flies before him! And shall we, who are creatures so mean and so vile, be careless and unconcerned, when we make the nearest approach to this great and holy God, that we can make on this side [of] heaven!

Ought we not to go blushing, ashamed and deeply humbled on many accounts, and particularly for our ingratitude for redeeming love, that love which passeth knowledge; and for our contempt of God's unspeakable gift, the greatest sin in the world; yea, we should go wondering that we are out of hell, for many thousands are burning there, who have not sinned so heinously in making light of precious Christ as we have done.

Did we always bear in our minds, that sacramental occasions are solemn appointments, and Bethel-meetings with God, for renewing covenant, and entertaining fellowship and communion with Him, we would guard more against formality creeping in upon us in our preparations for, and in our attendance upon this ordinance, than, alas, we do. Oh, such formality will provoke the Master of our solemn feasts to withdraw from them, and then what poor, dry, melancholy and lifeless things will they be? What are sacraments without Christ's presence in them? O let us never be satisfied with communion-sabbaths, without communion with Christ in them.

On the other hand, if we would keep up communion with Christ in these ordinances, let us beware of relying on our previous pains or preparations, either for our right performing of our duty, or for our acceptance in it: For we are never more ready to miscarry, and to be disappointed, than when we are guilty of this resting. Sundry [various people] go to the Lord's Table with great humiliation for sin, and yet come away without comfort. Why? because they make a Christ of their sorrow. — O what worth can we see in our best preparations, confessions, prayers, tears, humiliations, etc. if we compare them with the law of God? We have more cause to be ashamed of them, than to lay any stress on them. Could we renounce all self-confidence, and disclaim all our provision in point of dependence, and cast ourselves wholly on Christ for strength, thro'-bearing [endurance] and acceptance, we would have better success at the Lord's Table, than commonly we have.

We are never more fit for this holy Table, than when we are most humbled, and most ashamed of ourselves.

**Willison, *Sacramental Meditations*, iii–vii**

### Turning away from earthly riches

Wherefore do I spend my money for that which is not bread? And my labour for that which can never satisfy? Many a time have I made trial of the things that are visible, but the higher my expectations have been raised, the greater has been my disappointment. I have sought that among the creatures which is not to be found. Sin has turned this world into a country, far from God; and truly husks are the best fare that ever this world hath yielded me. 'Tis high time to come out from the world and to be separate, lest my soul perish for hunger there. Meat that perishes is improper for a soul that is of an immortal nature, and of an everlasting duration. I will arise and go unto my God and Father: He has promised to satiate and replenish the weary and sorrowful soul. In His house I am sure there is bread enough and to spare.

Boast not O mammon of thy treasures! Unless thou hast that which is of sufficient value to be a ransom for me. Can all the wealth of both the Indies pay the debt which by sin I have contracted? Can riches satisfy for the wrong I have done to the justice of God by my transgression? Oh no, I was not redeemed with corruptible things as silver and gold, but with the precious blood of Christ as of a lamb without blemish and without spot.

Lord! Thou who art full of love, nay love itself, and art jealous of my love lest it should be misplaced; turn away my eyes that they may not be set upon that which is not. If riches take to themselves wings and fly away as an eagle towards heaven; let my heart be so wise, as to get the start of them [that is, beat them to it], and fly away first from such transitory and fading vanities, and fly towards the highest heaven of all. How great a gain will it be to lose my love to the world! And though it be no gain at all to Thee for me to love Thee, who art so self-sufficient from everlasting to everlasting; yet I shall hereby be an eternal gainer, and shall be interested in that love which is everlasting and unchangeable. Oh! Love me freely in the Son of Thy love; and inflame my heart with love to Thee!

**Vincent, 273–74, 276**

## Despising man's honours

What is the applause and esteem of men! How vain and poor a thing is worldly honour! Why should I envy this to others, or be eager after it, or proud of it myself? Man does judge according to outward appearance, and therefore may more easily mistake. When man commends, conscience may condemn, and God much more. That which is highly esteemed among men is an abomination in the sight of God.

To be spoken well of by sinners is rather a bad sign; they were false prophets who had the good word of all men. And the good word of saints, is rather an argument of their charity, than of our sincerity. The Jew that is one inwardly, his heart is circumcized, and his praise not of men but of God.

How poor a thing is it to be praised for beauty, which is so great a snare to them that have it, and to others also; and which death may so quickly turn into paleness and rottenness!

And to be praised for worldly greatness, does yield but a sorry satisfaction for death is a sure and terrible leveller, and the worms will make as bold with the carcasses of the prince as of the peasant.

What will it advantage one to be commended for gifts, or parts [abilities], or grace, if conscience at the same time do justly reproach, and call one proud and hypocritical!

How little did Christ value honour in the days of His humiliation, He was despised, rejected, reproached and at last most ignominiously crucified. Lord! They are truly honourable, that honour Thee, and are honoured by Thee, and to whom Thou wilt say at last, 'Well done good and faithful servants.'

**Vincent, 280–82**

## Longing to sup with Christ

One must first of all endeavor to stir up *a strong desire* to be among God's people, to appear before the Lord. 'One thing have I desired of the LORD, that will I seek after; that I may dwell in the house of the LORD all the days of my life, to behold the beauty of the LORD, and to inquire in His temple' (Ps. 27:4); 'My soul thirsteth for God, for the living God: when shall I come and appear before God?' (Ps. 42:2).

The meeting place where the Lord's Supper is administered is at that moment none other than a portal of heaven — with Jacob one may say of it, 'Surely the LORD is in this place … How dreadful is this place! This is none other but the house of God, and this is the gate of heaven' (Gen. 28:16-17). Heaven opens itself in such a place, and the rays of divine glory and grace descend to that place, filling it with the very presence of God. The Father comes to His people with His favor and reveals Himself in a familiar manner to His favorites, addressing them as *Ammi, ruhamah!* that is, My people, and object of My mercy! I have loved thee with an everlasting love and therefore I have drawn thee with loving kindness. I have come here to meet you in order to make known to you, and to cause you to feel my delight and my love. The Lord Jesus, the

Bridegroom, comes in His love to them to have this Supper with them and to cause them to enjoy it together with Him. With love and delight He views them as they surround Him. It is there that the Holy Spirit is active, filling the soul with light, grace, and comforts.

Here is the household of God, and here spiritual friends are gathered together for a moment in order to delight themselves in the presence of their heavenly Father and in Jesus, their beloved Bridegroom. Whose heart, upon observing these manifestations, would not be stirred also to go there, to be part of this gathering, and also to delight oneself in the Lord? Even a barren soul will say, 'There I wish to go, for it could be that I may receive a blessing there.'

[C]onsider for a moment the sweet and friendly invitation of the Lord Jesus Himself. He has no need of you; He could have passed you by and have invited others. However, He now says to you, 'Come, for all things are ready!' This invitation He accompanies with so many sweet motives — yes, in His Name He beseeches you that you would come to Him. Furthermore, He Himself stands at the door and knocks, waiting for you to open to Him in order that He may sup with you and you with Him (Rev. 3:20). Since He calls and invites you in such a friendly manner to have fellowship with Him, would you then yet walk away or remain standing? No, but allow your heart to be set aflame with love for such a gathering, and let your soul, so to speak, fly there with wings.

**Brakel, 572–75**

## Seeking grace with a thirsty soul

'Ho, every one that thirsteth' [Isa. 55:1]. In that he calleth none to partake of the holy things of God, but those that are thus affected. The doctrine is: that, the thirsty soul alone hath interest in the graces of God, and shall reap benefit by the means of grace.

Those only that feel their own barrenness and emptiness, and highly esteem and heartily desire the mercies of God, through the merits of Christ, they only, I say, have right unto, and shall have a portion in the same. Therefore when David would move God to bring him again to the assemblies of the saints, where he might enjoy the means of comfort and of salvation, he useth this as a forcible argument, 'My soul thirsteth for God, for the living God: when shall I come and appear before God' (Ps. 42:2), and again, 'My soul longeth, yea, even fainteth for the courts of the LORD' (Ps. 84:2).

Now the reasons of this point are these:

First, no man hath any warrant to resort unto the means of godliness, but only such as were before mentioned [in Isaiah 55]: for thus the Lord inviteth men unto Him, 'Let him that is athirst, come. And whosoever will (namely, that is so qualified), let him take the water of life freely' (Rev. 22:17): so that none are bidden guests but such as have thirsty souls.

Second, none else have any promise of speeding well, if they should come: for thus goeth the promise, 'I will pour water upon him that is thirsty, and floods upon the dry ground' (Isa. 44:3). Till then, we can never have assurance of any benefit by God's ordinance: but when once we come with a longing heart, that doth as it were gape and enlarge itself to take in the rain of grace, as the dry ground doth to receive the showers that fall upon it, then though we be never so thirsty, we shall be full satisfied.

Thirdly, as those that are destitute of this spiritual thirst, have no commandment, nor promise from God: so neither have they any fitness in themselves, because they want [lack] that principal grace, which doth fit men for the entertaining of God's Holy Spirit (which alone maketh God's ordinance effectual), to wit, humility; which proceedeth from a sense of our own misery, and a sight of God's mercy.

In which regard it standeth us upon [or obliges us] to look unto our hearts beforehand: and to the intent that we may come with this spiritual appetite, the want whereof is so offensive unto God, and dangerous unto us, let us use all good means for the obtaining of it: as

First, to purge away that which may annoy our stomach and kill our appetite: and what that is, Peter telleth us when he said, 'Wherefore laying aside all malice, and all guile, and hypocrises, and envies, and all evil speakings, as newborn babes, desire the sincere milk of the word' [1 Peter 2:2]. As if he had said, so long as you give place unto, and delight in any evil, so long you can never delight in, or be very desirous of the pure Word of God.

A second is, that we must endeavor to know our own misery, what we are by nature, and by desert, in regard of our great and grievous offenses: that being so poor in spirit, we may sigh and cry for grace, whereas those that are proud in spirit care not for it.

Especially (if in the third place), we consider the excellency [of grace]: how it bringeth with it freedom from all evil: both from the guilt of sin, and from the power and punishment of sin: and withal, the enjoyment of all blessings needful for body or soul, for this life, or that which is to come. If (I say) the settled meditation hereof do not once sink into our hearts, it cannot but set our affections on fire, with an ardent and earnest desire of the same. Nothing makes us so weak and cold in hearing the Word, or communicating [sharing] of the sacrament, as that we have not sufficiently tasted how good the Lord is.

**Dod, 141–42, 144–45**

# 5

## PRAYERS OF PREPARATION

*Tremble, thou earth, at the presence of the Lord,*
*at the presence of the God of Jacob*
(Psalm 114:7).

### Approaching the Throne of Grace

O eternal and most blessed God, the fountain of being and bliss; infinite in perfection; and highly exalted above all our words or thoughts. I am astonished at the thoughts of the brightness of Thy glory: and justly afraid to present myself before so great and holy a Majesty. Even that abundant grace which invites me to Thee, abases me too; when I reflect upon my shameful ingratitude to such undeserved love.

I have done so much evil, and so little good; been so eager in the pursuit of the things of this world, and so cold and unconcerned many times about those of eternity; so unmindful of my promises, unthankful for Thy benefits, and unfruitful in the knowledge of the Lord Jesus: that it is a wonder of Thy patience, that I am still alive, and not cut down like a barren tree that cumbers the ground.

I know the sacrifices of the Lord are a broken spirit: a broken and a contrite heart, O God, Thou wilt not despise. And Jesus hath also offered Himself a sacrifice for us, in whom Thou hast declared that Thou art well pleased. For Jesus' sake dispose me now to offer unto Thee that acceptable sacrifice. And give me grace ever to fear Thee, and to walk humbly with Thee; to preserve a tender sense of my duty towards Thee, and conscientiously to obey Thee, that so, by virtue of His sacrifice of Himself, all my sins may be done away and remembered no more.

And now that I am going to Thy holy Table, to commemorate the sacrifice of my Saviour; to give Thee farther testimonies of my love to Thee, and receive new tokens of Thy love to me: O Lord, vouchsafe to make Thy self powerfully present to my mind. Represent Thy self and Thy Son Jesus so lively to my thoughts, in all Thy wisdom, power, goodness, holiness, and truth; that I may never forget Thee any more: but most furiously [strongly] reverence Thee; and love Thee, and rejoice in Thee, and trust Thee and obey Thee, all the days of my life.

And for that end, compose mine unsettled thoughts, before I approach to receive the holy mysteries. That I may attend Thee with a full and clear conception of their meaning; with an actual belief of Thy whole gospel; with most sensible love to Thee, and desire to be more like Thee; with Thy high praises in my mouth, and joy unspeakable in mine heart. May I presume, most gracious Father, to ask such tastes and relishes of Thy wondrous love, that I may never be able to delight in anything so much as in the remembrance of it. But mine eyes may be ever towards the Lord; and I may hunger and thirst perpetually after Thy righteousness, till I am perfectly made partaker of Thy divine nature, and rendered meet to be translated to that high and holy place, where I shall see Thee, (not as now in mysterious representations, but) openly, and face to face. Amen, Lord Jesus: who are able to save to the uttermost all them that come to God by Thee.

Patrick, *The Christian Sacrifice*, 138–44

## Receiving a broken Christ into a broken heart

Most holy, and blessed, and gracious Lord God, with all humility and reverence, I here present myself before Thee, to seek Thy face and entreat Thy favour, and, as an evidence of Thy good-will towards me, to beg that I may experience Thy good work in me.

I acknowledge myself unworthy, utterly unworthy of the honour; unfit, utterly unfit for the service to which I am now called. It is an inestimable privilege, that I am permitted so often to hear from Thee in Thy word, and to speak to Thee in prayer: and yet, as if this had been a small matter, I am now invited into communion with Thee at Thy holy Table, there to celebrate the memorial of my Saviour's death, and to partake by faith of the precious benefits which flow from it. I who deserve not the crumbs, am called to eat the children's bread.

Lord, I confess I have sinned against Thee, I have done foolishly, very foolishly, for foolishness is bound up in my heart. I have sinned, and have come short of being glorified with Thee. The imagination of my heart is evil continually, and the bias of my corrupt nature is very strong toward the world, and the flesh, and the gratifications of sense; but towards God, and Christ, and heaven, I move slowly, and with a great many stops and pauses. Nay, there is in my carnal mind a wretched aversion to divine and spiritual things. I have misspent my time, trifled away my opportunities, have followed after lying vanities, and forsake my own mercies. God be merciful to me a sinner! For how little have I done, since I came into the world, of the great work that I was sent into the world about?

Thou hast taken me into covenant with Thee, for I am a baptized Christian, set apart for Thee, and sealed to be Thine; Thou has laid me, and I also have laid myself under all possible obligations to love Thee, and serve Thee, and live to Thee. But I have started [or turned] aside from Thee like a deceitful bow, I have not made good my covenant with Thee, nor hath the temper of my mind, and the tenor of my conversation [or conduct] been agreeable to that holy religion which I make profession of, to my expectations from Thee, and engagements to Thee. I am bent to backslide from the living God; and if I were under the law I were undone; but I am under grace, a covenant of grace which leaves room for repentance, and promiseth pardon upon repentance, which invites even backsliding children to return, and promises that their backslidings shall be healed.

Lord, I take hold of this covenant, seal it to me at Thy Table. There let me find my heart truly humbled for sin, and sorrowing for it after a godly sort: O that I may there look on Him whom I have pierced, and mourn, and be in bitterness for Him; that there I may sow in tears, and receive a broken Christ into a broken heart: and there let the blood of Christ, which speaks better things than that of Abel, be sprinkled upon my conscience, to purify and pacify that. There let me be assured that Thou art reconciled to me, that my iniquities are pardoned, and that I shall not come into condemnation. There say unto me, be of good cheer, thy sins are forgiven thee.

And that I may not come unworthily to this blessed ordinance, I beseech Thee lead me into a more intimate and experimental acquaintance with Jesus Christ and Him crucified; with Jesus Christ and Him glorified; that knowing Him, and the power of His resurrection, and the fellowship of His sufferings, and being by His grace planted in the likeness of both, I may both discern the Lord's body, and show forth the Lord's death.

Lord, I desire by a true and lively faith to close with [come to] Jesus Christ, and consent to Him as my Lord, and my God; I here give up myself to Him as my Prophet, Priest, and King, to be ruled, and taught, and saved by Him; this is my beloved, and this is my friend. None but Christ, none but Christ. Lord, increase this faith in me, perfect what is lacking in it; and enable me, in receiving the bread and wine at Thy Table, by a lively faith to receive Christ Jesus the Lord. O let the great gospel doctrine of Christ's dying to save sinners, which is represented in that ordinance, be meat and drink to my soul, meat indeed, and drink indeed. Let it be both nourishing and refreshing to me, let it be both my strength and my song, and be the spring both of my holiness and my comfort. And let such deep impressions be made upon my soul, by actual commemoration of it, as may abide always upon me, and have a powerful influence upon me in my whole conversation, that the life I now live in the flesh, I may live by the faith of the Son of God, who loved me, and gave himself for me.

Work in me (I pray Thee) a principle of holy love and charity towards all men, that I may forgive my enemies (which by grace I heartily do) and may keep up a spiritual communion in faith, hope, and holy love, with all that in every place call on the name of Jesus Christ our Lord. Lord, bless them all, and particularly that congregation with which I am to join in this solemn ordinance.

**Henry, *Method for Prayer*, 241–45**

## Melt my heart with the fire of Thy love

O holy and merciful Saviour, merciful beyond example, who treatest me as Thy child, hast prepared a Table for me, and made my cup run over!

Be Thou my Shepherd, let me want no grace, no mercy, no assistance that's necessary for me in the prosecuting of mine eternal happiness. Dress me with Thy robes, adorn me with the ensigns of Thy favour. Let me rejoice at the Supper Thou hast prepared for me. Teach me to entertain Thy call with gladness. Let me see clearly what Thou hast prepared for them that love Thee.

Thou knowest my stubborn and lazy heart, rouse it from its slumber; melt it by the fire of Thy love; breathe upon these dry bones, and they shall live: Let me not with Esau prefer a morsel of bread, eaten in secret before my birth-right to eternal glory.

Let me consider Thy condescension, in inviting such a wretch to sup with Thee. Let not the evil examples I see before me be any temptation to me. Uphold me by Thy right hand. Let me dread Thine anger, and count it a greater disgrace to be despised by Thee, than to be made the filth and off-scouring of all things. Give me a just esteem of Thy favour, let me prefer it before all the contents of this present world. Let me feel that Thy loving-kindness is better than life; this life will fade away, but Thy mercy endureth for ever. Let goodness and mercy follow me all the days of my life, and make me dwell in Thy house for ever. Amen.

**Horneck, 13**

### Give me a lively and vigorous faith

Almighty and most merciful God, who will be sanctified in them that come nigh Thee, I beseech Thee to prepare my heart for that solemn ordinance, in which I have such near access unto Thee by Jesus Christ.

Give unto me, I pray Thee, all needful and suitable graces, and tempers, that in partaking of the bread and wine, according to the institution of my Lord and Saviour, and in remembrance of His death, I may truly have the communion of His body and blood.

I desire to see, and to feel, the plague of my own evil heart; and to come, weary and heavy laden under the burden of my many sins, to Jesus Christ for pardon and relief. May I be enabled, in the celebration of this institution, to keep in view Jesus Christ, and Him crucified. 'May I enjoy here not only a representation, but a rich participation also, of His dying love.' Give me a lively and vigorous faith in Him, that I may entirely rely on His merits for acceptance with Thee, and depend on Him alone for the supply of all my spiritual wants. Bring all needful things to my remembrance, and keep from me those things that would distract and disturb my devotion.

Deliver me from the evil and danger of eating and drinking unworthily, that I may not bring down judgements instead of blessings. Put away far from me all ignorance, irreverence, and want of charity. Let me not be under the influence of a carnal, self-righteous, and worldly spirit: lest in any measure I become a sharer in the sin of those who are guilty of the body and blood of Christ.

Give me, also, I pray Thee, all the benefits which my Saviour did, by this institution, design to convey to His people. Teach me to discern therein the Lord's body, and vouchsafe to me a large measure of Thy grace, that my remembrance of Christ may be serious and impressive, and may produce an increase of penitence, faith, gratitude, and holy obedience. Make Thyself known to me, O Jesus, in the breaking of bread. May the Holy Ghost produce in me a composed, tranquil, and devout spirit at Thy Table. I desire there, O heavenly Father, to celebrate the death of Christ as a sacrifice taking away the sin of the world, and the only foundation of every spiritual hope. I desire, while commemorating His death, to remember His risen glory, and to declare my expectation of His coming again to judge the world, and save His people. I pray that I may find His death made efficacious to the mortification of all my sins.

O that it may please Thee that pardon, justification, peace with God, sanctification, the hope of eternal life, and all the blessings which Christ, by His death, hath obtained for us, may now be afresh conveyed and assured to me through faith in Him. Give me a sweet sense of communion with all true believers, and of our common union to Christ, the head of His Church, and our fellowship with Him and with each other. Thus may love to Christ, and love to all the brethren, be greatly strengthened and increased among us. O may we all thus experience the Lord's Supper to be a refreshing means of grace, so that we may return from Thy Table 'with our consciences quieted, our corruptions subdued, our graces increased, and our soul encouraged, with an enlarged heart to run the way of Thy commandments'.

Increase the number of faithful communicants throughout Thy churches in all the world; and enlarge the borders of Thy kingdom, till all the ends of the earth remember the Saviour's sufferings, and turn to the Lord and worship before Thee. This I ask, for His name's sake. Amen.

**Bickersteth, 192–94**

## Holy Jesus, raise up our minds to Thee

Holy Jesus, presence Thyself [that is, make Thy presence known] with us, and raise up our minds to Thy blessed self. Let us converse with Thee. Open to our view the mysteries of Thy person, love, blood, and death. We sing Thy praise now, and will when we come to Thy Table, to feed on the sacred memorials of Thy body and blood, for what Thou hast been, done, and suffered on our behalf, as the author of our eternal salvation. We sing Thy praise for loving us, and washing us from our sins in Thy blood. Glory and honor, and blessing and praise we desire, under the influence of Thy Holy Spirit, to offer up unto Thee for Thy most precious, finished, and eternal salvation; and for Thy obedience and sufferings, by which Thou didst obtain it.

Glory to Thee, O Lord Jesus Christ, for Thine obedience unto death, even the death of the cross. We praise Thee, for Thy sorrows, we bless Thee, that Thou wast exceeding sorrowful, even unto death. O for such a sense of what Thou didst endure in Thy mind, when our sins beset Thee, when they encompassed Thee, when they stared Thee in the face, and were so felt by Thee, as caused Thee to be full of heaviness, and filled Thy holy soul with amazement, as may endear Thee to our souls for ever. We praise Thee, Thou blessed Jesus, for

Thine agony and soul-travail, for Thy sweating a bloody sweat to make us clean from all sin. We would, O Lord Jesus, take our standing at Thy cross, and say, Unto Thee that loved us, and washed us from our sins in Thine own blood, be glory and dominion for ever and ever. Amen. Thy bloody-sweat is our everlasting cure — the fountain of health and purity. Blessed be Thy holy name, by Thine agony and bloody sweat in the garden, Thou hast proved Thy love to us, Thou hast washed us thereby from our sins, in Thine own most precious blood.

We thank Thee, that Thou gavest Thy body to be wounded, and that with Thy stripes we are healed. We praise Thee for giving Thy back to the smiters, and Thy cheeks to them that plucked off the hair, that Thou didst not hide Thy face from shame and spitting. All praise is due to Thee for wearing a crown of thorns, for being nailed to the tree, that our heads might be crowned with crowns of glory, and that we might be set at everlasting liberty. For whom Thou makest free, they are free indeed.

Lord Jesus, create in our minds, from Thy Word and by Thy Spirit, some precious apprehensions of Thy soul-sufferings, of Thy enduring the curse, and making Thy soul an offering for sin, as may fill our souls with wonder, love, and praise to Thy holy name continually. May we join Thy whole church on earth and in heaven, ever more praising Thee, and saying, 'Unto him that loved us, and washed us from our sins in his own blood, and hath made us kings and priests unto God and his Father: to him be glory and dominion forever and ever. Amen.'

Go with us, Lord Jesus, to Thy holy Table. Shine on the bread, shine on the cup. Give us to feed and feast on Thee. Open our hearts afresh to receive Thee — and open Thine heart afresh to the view of our faith. Let us have some sure and certain token of Thy presence with us. Let us be satisfied with Thy goodness. Even so let it be, O Lord Jesus Christ, for Thy name and mercies sake. Amen.

**Pierce, 443–445**

# PART II
# FEASTING AT THE TABLE

# 6

## REMEMBERING CHRIST CRUCIFIED

*Take, eat: this is my body, which is broken for you:*
*this do in remembrance of me… This cup is the new testament*
*in my blood: this do ye, as oft as ye drink it,*
*in remembrance of me*
(1 Corinthians 11:24-25).

### In remembrance of Him, showing forth His death

What Christ calls 'doing in remembrance of him', the apostle, the best interpreter of His words, styles 'shew[ing] the Lord's death' (1 Cor. 11:26). So that His death is the thing that is to be remembered here by all the communicants.

1.  It was *the death of God.* The death remembered here is the death of the King of kings; and though as God, He could not die, yet it may truly be said that He that was God, did die, not in His Godhead, but in His humanity.

2. It was *the death of a Person*, higher than the highest, for His enemies. Here a Person adored by angels, worshipped by all the host of heaven, the comfort of Paradise, the joy of seraphim, the terror of devils, the Lord of life, the eternal Son of God, the brightness of His Father's glory, and the express image of His Person, dies for men, for men miserable and wretched, for men that were sinners, for men that were proper objects of His justice, for men that were haters of God, acted like enemies, had affronted their Maker, crucified their Redeemer, came out against Him, as against a thief, who took pleasure in trampling on His laws, rejoiced in their disobedience for such this wonderful Person dies, and this makes His death miraculous and astonishing (Rom. 5:8).

3. It's *a death that nature and all the elements were confounded at*. The sun hid his face, that he might not see his Creator die; the earth trembled, as if it were ashamed to see men stupid [senseless] at the dreadful spectacle; the rocks broke. The veil of the temple was rent.

4. It is *a death, whereby the Person suffering merited eternal life*, not only for Himself, but all His followers too. It was for His death that the everlasting Father exalted Christ's human nature above powers, angels, principalities, and spiritual creatures; and in doing so, declared, what those, whose nature He had assumed, if they did follow Him in the regeneration, might come to after death, viz. eternal life and glory. To see God, and to be ravished with His sight forever; to enjoy riches, honor, glory, power, dominion, pleasure, recreation, houses, lands, in a most eminent manner. In that death all these treasures are amassed and heaped, and piled up together, and

then it may be worth remembering; nay, it is impossible not to remember it, where all this is believed.

**Horneck, 155–59**

## Remembering is more than reciting history

How can we, removed centuries from the scenes of that memorable night, who did not see, or hear, or feel, what they saw, and heard, and felt — how can we remember Him in this ordinance, as they were commanded to remember Him?

How? By faith; by a realizing faith. All faith is not realizing faith. A mere mental belief in the record of Christ's sufferings and death is faith — faith that is necessary to salvation, but not the realizing faith which brings salvation into the soul. The merely nominal believer acknowledges the truth of the sacred history, that the man, Christ Jesus, was born of the virgin Mary, suffered under Pontius Pilate, was crucified, dead, and buried, and that He rose again from the dead on the third day, and ascended into heaven. But more than this is implied in the requirement, 'This do in remembrance of me.'

This merely intellectual belief is, indeed, sometimes accompanied by strong impulses of feeling. We naturally sympathize with the suffering victim of cruelty. Fiction itself has this power over us, when there is not a particle of faith in the reality of the things represented.

Precisely here communicants are most liable to be deceived. They meditate upon Christ's sufferings until their feelings are overwhelmed with the view they have of them; and they leave the Table of the Lord in a state of mind which they mistake for increased devotion and spirituality.

If we have received Christ by faith, we have had a realizing sense of His power and grace, as our atoning Redeemer, to save us from sin. It was at the moment our faith beheld Him on the cross, crucified for us and for the world, that we felt the evidence of pardon and peace with God through Him. Such is the experience of all who are truly converted to God. It was then that Christ crucified became the object of the heart's supreme affections. His image was impressed upon it. He was the joy and the song of our new-born souls by day and by night. No object was so lovely, none so endeared to the heart, as the suffering Saviour, seen by faith upon the cross. It was His love, manifested by His passion and death, that rendered Him supremely lovely to the believing heart. 'Unto you therefore which believe he is precious' (1 Peter 2:7).

**Luckey, 57–62**

## Signs for the senses, Christ for the soul

If we consider the Supper as a sign, given us for instruction, it exhibits a remembrance of Christ, and a lively representation of most of the awful mysteries of our religion, as the Greek fathers often speak. The bread signifies the body of Christ. For, as bread strengtheneth man's heart (Ps. 104:15), so the flesh of Christ, and the spiritual blessings and graces purchased for us by Christ, when He was incarnate, are the food of our soul, supporting and strengthening it in the spiritual life, into the hope of life eternal. 'I am the living bread which came down from heaven: if any man eat of this bread, he shall live for ever:

and the bread that I will give is my flesh, which I will give for the life of the world' (John 6:51). Again, as corn, from which bread is prepared, is ground to meal, kneaded to dough, and baked in the oven, before it can be agreeable and wholesome food for man; so in like manner, the Captain of our salvation was made perfect through various sufferings (Heb. 2:10), and scorched both in the fire of the divine wrath kindled against our sins, and in the flames of His own love.

The wine signifies the blood of Christ. For, as wine allays the thirst, revives the spirits, cheers the heart (Ps. 104:15; Prov. 31:6-7) so in like manner, the grace purchased by the blood of Christ allays the thirst of our soul, abundantly satisfying all our holy longings (John 4:14), to a kind of a holy and mystical ebriety [or intoxication] (Ps. 36:8; Song 5:1), it supports and sustains the soul when sick of love (Song 2:5), and puts 'gladness in my heart, more than in the time that their corn and their wine are increased' (Ps. 4:7). And we must not omit, that as wine is squeezed with much force from the grapes, when trodden in the wine press; so in like manner the Lord Jesus was straitened [or distressed] (Luke 12:50), and oppressed with much anguish, that the blood might flow to us from His blessed body, and His spiritual grace with His blood.

When the dispenser of the mysteries of God takes the bread and the cup of blessing into his hands, before the eyes of the faithful, that seems to intimate, that Christ was thus constituted and taken to be Mediator, and set forth to believers, 'to be a propitiation through faith in his blood' (Rom. 3:25). The blessing and thanksgiving pronounced over the bread and wine teach us that Christ is that blessed seed of Abraham, in whom 'God ... hath blessed us with all spiritual blessings in heavenly places' (Eph. 1:3), and the greatest gift of divine bounty, for which to all eternity we shall not be able to render suitable thanks. The breaking of the bread represents the breaking of Christ's body, especially that by death; for, the soul is the band, by which all the parts of the body are preserved united. The pouring out of the wine represents the shedding of Christ's blood, that especially which was done on the cross, for the confirmation of the New Testament. And thus in the holy Supper there is a commemoration of the death of Christ, not in words only, but also by those mystical rites. The distribution of these sacred pledges is a figure or emblem of that gratuitous offer, by which the Lord Jesus, with all His saving benefits, is presented to the elect, with the most alluring invitations to accept of Him: nor offered only, but actually reached out, and freely given to believers for their eternal salvation.

But when believers receive the bread and wine, they declare by that action, that they receive by a true faith Christ Himself, and all He is, that they may have a right to become the sons of God (John 1:12). But the eating the bread and drinking the wine signify something more. And first, they really set forth the devout and lively employment of the soul, engaged in holy meditations on Christ, who is all its desire, that it may derive from Him everything it knows to be needful for its spiritual life. Again, these actions also signify that intimate union which subsists between Christ and believers: as meat and drink, when put into the mouth, are not only received into the stomach, but also converted into the very substance of the person. This union the Scripture calls an abode (John 14:23), a joining (1 Cor. 6:17), the same body (Eph. 3:6). Lastly, they represent that sweetest delight which the hungry and thirsty soul enjoys from the fruition of Christ and His grace: not only believing, but seeing and tasting, that the Lord is good (Ps. 34:9; 1 Peter 2:3). And as all are partakers of one bread and of one wine, this is a figure of that amicable unity, whereby they who partake of the same sacred feast, are united together, as domestics of the same Lord: 'For we being many are one bread, and one body: for we are all partakers of that one bread' (1 Cor. 10:17).

**Witsius, 459–62**

## Take, eat, sincerely, fully, personally

Q. What is the import of these words concerning the bread: 'take, eat'?

A. It is as if Christ had said, 'Receive and make use of this broken bread as a sign and seal of My broken body, with all its benefits. As you take the bread out of My hand, and by eating it receive it into your stomachs, so accept a Savior as He is offered unto you; receive the atonement, approve of it and consent to it; come up to the gracious terms on which Christ and His benefits are proposed to you; accept His grace and submit to His government.'

Q. What should we think upon when we hear these words?

A. We should think upon the infinite free love of God in giving His Son, and of Christ in giving Himself to such poor wretches as we are. Yes, we should, in a contemplative and believing way, think we see Christ (as it were personally) at the head of the Table, making offer of Himself to us in the freest manner, saying, 'Take Me, and the whole purchase of death and sufferings; take My sealed testament, and all the legacies in it; take a sealed pardon of all your sins, and a sealed right to eternal life.'

Q. In what manner are we to take Christ and His benefits in this sacrament?

A. We are to take Christ and all the blessings of His covenant in the following manner:

1. Sincerely and honestly, without hypocrisy, which is a thing most hated by God.

2. Entirely, fully, and without exception of anything required of us.

3. With close and particular application, saying, 'My Lord and my God.'

4. With thanksgiving and praise, stirring up our souls and all that is within us to bless His holy name. Bless God for such a glorious Surety, such a rich purchase, such a free covenant, and such suitable promises.

5. With humility and self-denial, reckoning ourselves unworthy of the least crumb from His Table, renouncing all confidence in our preparations, humiliations, or qualifications of any sort, and saying, 'In the Lord only have we righteousness and strength.'

6. We ought to take Christ and His purchase in the sacrament with full assurance of faith — looking on the sacramental bread as the Lord's seal and pledge of our interest in and title to all the blessings of the covenant; taking this bread as a sure sign and token from Christ that His body was broken for us; and believing that Christ and all the blessings

of the covenant and purchase of His death are here given to us as really as Christ gives the bread into our hands.

**Willison, *Sacramental Catechism*, 89–91**

## Our public confession of Christ crucified

This ordinance is *speculum crucifixi* [a mirror of the Crucified], as Calvin saith. It is the business of the communicant to show forth this death of the Lord. The ordinance itself is full of death, what other language doth bread broken, and the blood severed from the body, speak but a dying Christ. As the ordinance, so the communicant doth by eating and drinking, in fact declare and annunciate his profession of adherence to, and embracement of the death of Christ, we solemnly and publicly avow, both to God and men, that we stick unto, and abide by the death of the Lord, for the remission of sin, and reconciliation of our persons to God; and it is a solemn part of God's positive worship, to show forth the death of Christ our Lord, not by a mere historical relation, but a practical and public profession of our faith, and acceptance thereof, which though at all times we may remember, yet God would have a solemn ordinance in His gospel-churches, for the commemoration and showing of it forth, which ordinance is this of the Supper. I know men are witty to elude ordinances, and to flatter themselves with private devotions and meditations, but when God hath set up an ordinance in purpose, for the public and solemn showing of the Lord's death; let them consider it, that are not only careless of the benefit of it, but fail of their duty, by not presenting themselves at this solemn showing of the Lord's death.

The use of the point is to call upon all communicants, to be intent upon, and taken up with this employment. Show ye forth the Lord's death, this must be your actual exercise at the time of eating and drinking, the death of Christ must fill your eyes, your ears, your lips, your thoughts. If any of you could see Christ dying, the sight would wholly take you up; and you come as near to see Him dying, as an ordinance can bring you, in a representation. If anywhere, that takes place here, 'Rejoice with trembling' (Ps. 2:11). Tremble, for you see the weight of sin upon the Lord Christ, and the severity and wrathful indignation of God against sin, both those terrors cannot be seen in a clearer glass, than the death of the Lord. Rejoice for the love that delivers up Christ is unparalleled, and the death of the Lord is succedaneous [a substitute in place of others], a sacrifice death, the sacrifice bears the sin, and takes it off you.

**Vines, 167–70**

# 7

# LAYING YOUR SINS AT THE FOOT
# OF THE CROSS

*For this is my blood of the new testament, which is shed for*
*many for the remission of sins*
(Matthew 26:28).

## Grieving over our sins that crucified Christ

In this sacrament, where it is designed that the eye should affect the heart, we must not rest in the bare contemplation of what is here set before us, but the consideration thereof must make an impression upon our spirits, which should be turned as wax to the seal. If what is here done do not affect us for the present, it will not likely to influence us afterwards; for we retain the remembrance of things better by our affections, than by our notions: 'I shall never forget thy precepts, when by them thou hast quickened me.' Here, therefore, let us stir up the gift that is in us, endeavouring to affect ourselves with the great things of God and our souls; and let us pray to God to affect us with them by His Spirit and grace.

Here we must be sorrowful for sin, after a godly sort, and blushing before God at the thought of it. Penitential grief and shame are not at all unsuitable to this ordinance, though it is intended for our joy and honour, but excellent preparatives for the benefit and comfort of it. Here we should be, like Ephraim, bemoaning ourselves; like Job, abhorring ourselves, renewing those sorrowful reflections we made upon our own follies, when we were preparing for this service, and keeping the fountain of repentance still open, still flowing. Our sorrow for sin needs not hinder our joy in God, and therefore our joy in God must not forbid our sorrow for sin.

I am here drawing nigh to God, not only treading His courts with Christians at large, but sitting down at His Table with select disciples; but when I consider how pure and holy He is, and how vile and sinful I am, I am ashamed, and blush to lift up my face before Him. To me belongs shame and confusion of face. I have many a time heard of God by the hearing of the ear, but now I am taken to sit down with Him at His Table. Mine eyes see Him, see the King in His beauty; wherefore I abhor myself, and repent in dust and ashes. — What a fool, what a wretch have I been, to offend a God who appears so holy in the eyes of all who draw nigh unto Him, and so great to all them that are about Him? Woe is me, for I am undone, lost and undone for ever, if there were not a Mediator between me and God, because I am a man of unclean lips and an unclean heart. Now I perceive it, and my own degeneracy and danger by reason of it, for mine eyes have seen the King, the Lord of hosts. I have reason to be ashamed to see One to whom I am so unlike, and afraid to see One to whom I am so obnoxious. The higher we are advanced by the free grace of God, the more reason we shall see to abase ourselves, and cry, 'God be merciful to us, sinners!'

A sight of Christ crucified should increase, excite our penitential shame and sorrow, and that evangelical repentance, in which there is an eye to the cross of Christ. It is prophesied, nay, it is promised, as a blessed effect of the pouring out of the Spirit, in gospel times, 'upon the house of David, and the inhabitants of Jerusalem … and they shall look on [him] whom they have pierced, and they shall mourn for him' [Zech. 12:10]. Here we see Christ pierced for our sins, nay, pierced by our sins: our sins were the cause of His death, and the grief of His heart. The Jews and Romans crucified Christ; but, as David killed Uriah with his letter, and Ahab killed Naboth with his seal; so the handwriting that was against us for our sins, nailed Christ to the cross, and so He nailed it to the cross. We had eaten the sour grapes, and His teeth were set on edge. Can we see Him thus suffering for us, and shall we not suffer with Him? Was He in such pain for us, and shall not we be in pain for Him? Was His soul exceeding sorrowful, even unto death, and shall not ours be exceeding sorrowful, when that is the way to life? Come, my soul, see by faith the holy Jesus made sin for thee; the glory of heaven made a reproach of men for thee; His Father's joy made a man of sorrow for thy transgressions.

**Henry,** ***Communicant's Companion,*** **199–203**

### Participating with reverence, holiness, and faith

We should show forth and remember this death:

#### 1. *Reverentially*

(1) With a reverence of the holiness of God. God's hatred of sin is as high as His love to Christ; He hates sin as much as He loves His Son. He would never else have dealt so hardly [harshly] with His Son for sin, whom He loved so dearly;

(2) With a reverence of the justice of God. It was more that the Son of God should thus pour out His soul, than if the whole world had been hurled into hell. God struck Him till justice had a full revenge, and struck Him with that wrath which would have tumbled us into unquenchable flames.

#### 2. *Holily*

(1) With mourning hearts for sin. A broken Christ must not be remembered without a broken heart; a bleeding Christ and a hardened spirit, a sighing Christ and a senseless heart, are unsuitable. Our Passover must be eaten with bitter herbs, with sorrow for past transgression;

(2) With deep considerations of the cursed nature and demerit of sin. It must needs be bitter, killing, condemning, cursed sin, which brought Christ to such a bitter death. Our iniquities met upon Him (Isa. 53:6), like a mighty torrent that bears down all before it; and who but infiniteness could have stood against such a force?

(3) With strong resolutions against sin. It is a sad thing to be Christians at a Supper, heathens in our shops, and devils in our closets. The Jews took the Passover standing, to show their intentions to leave Egypt; so we must resolve to leave all correspondence with those enemies which have murdered the Redeemer. The Passover must be eaten with unleavened bread; no leaven of sin must be mixed with our services, no leaven of hypocrisy with our lives (1 Cor. 5:7-8).

3. *Believingly*

(1) We should profess our adherence to Him. The showing forth [of] His death is solemnly to cleave to Him alone for the pardon of our sins, the justification of our persons, and the sanctification of our natures.

(2) Look up to Christ in His death as a conqueror. He was a King upon the cross as well as a Priest. He then nailed our sins to the cross; He then triumphed over the powers of darkness, sin, Satan, and hell (Col. 2:14-15).

(3) Plead this death with God. It is the best argument to prevail with God, who, though He may deny our prayers, will not deny His Son's blood. Present God with His covenant sealed: God will not deny His own hand and seal; present Him with this performance of Christ's priestly office, which is the only office He hath confirmed by an oath (Ps. 110:4).

(4) Plead this death against sin and Satan. Show it against every charge. Whatsoever accusation Satan can present against you is answered here. Have we sinned great sins? The

death of Christ for sin was the death of the Son of God. Can the sins of men be stronger to condemn than the blood of God is to save? We have deserved hell, but Christ hath suffered it.

**Charnock, 4:399–401**

### Confidence in a competent Saviour

Christ crucified is proposed unto us in the sacrament, as the object of our faith, alluring us to a firm belief in Him, upon these two strong persuasions:

1. That He is Saviour, all sufficient, having with Him plenteous redemption. One that hath paid the utmost farthing [less than a penny] that could be demanded for our ransom, having trodden the winepress of the fierce wrath of the Almighty, and borne upon His shoulders the whole burden of that vengeance, which would have sunk our souls to the bottom of hell. A Saviour that hath utterly defeated all the powers of darkness; and spoiled them, leading captivity captive: thereby purchasing for us a kingdom that cannot be shaken, but sure and steadfast against all violence of our spiritual adversaries, even a stable and firm estate in present grace, and an open and fair passage unto that immortality and glory which shall be revealed. Wherefore, justly hath He in this sacrament set forth Himself unto us, under the two elements of bread and wine, parts of one complete and perfect nourishment: to assure us, that in His merits, there is an absolute all-sufficiency to bring us to everlasting life.

2. That He is a Saviour freely given of God, and giving Himself unto us. He laid down His life freely, no man having

power to take it from Him: and therefore, He freely gave His flesh for the life of the world; and in the sacrament He freely offers Himself to every believer, to be received and embraced by him. Both these are strong motives to quicken our faith in remembering Christ's death: for if either the greatness of the work of redemption, and surpassing difficulty to save a sinner, should terrify us; we know whatever it be, He hath finished it: or if our unworthiness should discomfort us, we see that Christ stays [waits] not till we can deserve Him; but as He died for us when we were unworthy, so even while we are unworthy, He offers himself to us in all the benefits of His death. Wherefore let us in a lively faith fasten our eyes upon this brazen serpent, lifted up on the cross to cure the fiery stingings of sin: let our eyes, our thoughts, and our affections be drawn after Him, and learn we, as the Apostle exhorts, to trust perfectly unto that salvation which is brought unto us.

**Pemble, 11–12**

## Trusting in the sufficiency of His blood

How dismal is our case by nature! We are slaves to sin and Satan, and prisoners of the justice of God, being sentenced to die, doomed to wrath, and reserved to public judgement and execution. In this miserable condition were all mankind, until Christ came to ransom us. And O how difficult and costly was our redemption to Christ! No less could be the price of it, than His precious blood. The glorious Son of God who created heaven and earth, must become a creature, be born of a woman, and pour out His blood on an ignominious cross, before we could be redeemed from sin and wrath. In this blood I see sundry things.

1. The amazing love of Christ, in shedding His blood for the redemption of such creatures as I am; creatures most ugly, that had lost the image of God and got Satan's image picture in its room. Creatures, loathsome as dead carcasses, being dead in trespasses; and, yet these He loved so as to shed His blood.

2. In Christ's blood I see the glory of infinite wisdom displayed. Who could have found out a way to reconcile justice and mercy, and satisfy both their demands about Adam's fallen race? A general council of angels could never have thought of the Son of God's being made flesh and shedding blood!

3. This blood being the blood of God, hath infinite virtue and efficacy; it hath purchased the church of God, and all grace and glory. This blood is able to save to the uttermost.

4. I see this redeeming blood to be a suitable remedy for all my maladies. O that I could look to it by faith, apply it to my sores, and plead it with God:

> Lord, I am an unrighteous creature, but here is justifying blood; my heart is unholy, but here sanctifying blood; my soul is wounded, but here healing blood; my lusts are strong, but here mortifying blood; my heart is hard, but here softening blood; my affections are dead, but here quickening blood; my love is cold, but here is heart-warming blood. O my glorious bleeding Lamb, if Thou wilt, thou canst make me clean. O say to me, as Thou didst to the leper, 'I will, be thou clean.' Surely

Thy blood is more able to save me, than my sins are to destroy me.

**Willison, *Sacramental Meditations*, 76–80**

### Cheerfully coming to a reconciled Father in Christ

We should come with cheerful confidence in God, as our reconciled Father in Christ. As we are not going to hear our condemnation, but to receive our renewed acquittance and assurance of favor, we should approach in the character of children, should possess the confidence of children, with gladness and singleness of heart, coming to the Table where our Father gives the testimony of His regard to us. To come with slavish trembling and confusion to a feast of love, is utterly unseemly; and shows, either that we are unacquainted with the nature of the ordinance, or have not that faith that embraces the promises, and realizes the sign.

We must remember we are approaching a Table which love, eternal love, hath spread for sinners. That we have such a powerful Advocate for us entered into the heavens; that we may come boldly to the throne of grace, and not fear a disappointment. And that therefore in the strength of all this, we may without presumption, if we are really children of God, draw near with a true heart in full assurance of faith. This disposition is as honorable to God, as comfortable to ourselves, and most needful now to be exercised when every soul should rejoice and be exceeding glad, and triumph in the God of his salvation. When people come to the communion, as criminals to the bar [courtroom], it plainly shows they are still under the law, and are in bondage unto fear; that they have been resting in their own preparation, and their own worthiness, as though they must be in such a measure good, and they were afraid they had not arrived at the measure they proposed to themselves; thus making faith void and the promise to none effect. But believing souls (unless 'for a season, if need be, they be in heaviness through manifold temptations'), will be cheerful ones; they become humble, yet confident; serious, yet cheerful.

**Haweis, 75–76**

# 8

# RENEWING YOUR COVENANT WITH GOD

*And he took the book of the covenant, and read in the audience of the people: and they said, All that the LORD hath said will we do, and be obedient. And Moses took the blood, and sprinkled it on the people, and said, Behold the blood of the covenant, which the LORD hath made with you concerning all these words. Then went up Moses, and Aaron, Nadab, and Abihu, and seventy of the elders of Israel: and they saw the God of Israel: and there was under his feet as it were a paved work of a sapphire stone, and as it were the body of heaven in his clearness. And upon the nobles of the children of Israel he laid not his hand: also they saw God, and did eat and drink* (Exodus 24:7-11).

## Sharing in a covenant meal with God

The Lord's Supper is, in its own nature, a federal [covenantal] ordinance, which implies a covenant transaction between God and us and supposes a renewal of our vows to be the Lord's.

First, therefore, consider the mutual action in this ordinance of giving and taking between God and us, and you will see plain evidence in the nature of the thing of a covenant transaction. "Tis plain, simply bread and wine,' you'll say. And 'tis true, no more falls under the view of sense. But is it that is thereby signified? Is it not a bruised, nay, a broken Christ, giving His soul as an offering for sin, and shedding His blood to make atonement?

God gives Himself, His Son, His Spirit, His grace, His favor, and all that can be reasonably desired or truly wanted to the believing soul. This is on one side.

On the other side, the believer takes. With his hands he takes the distributed bread and wine, and receives with all his heart what is thereby portrayed and represented. He receives an offered Christ in his arms and into his heart. In short, God actually makes over, makes a delivery, as it were, of all that He promises in the covenant of grace on His part. We, by taking then what He gives, naturally engage to all that in that covenant He has made our duty.

'Behold,' says God there to all such persons, 'here's a Christ for you, to be taken by you, as your Prophet, Priest, and King.' Whereto the prepared soul naturally replies, 'Lord, I am ready to take Him as Thou offerest Him to me. I'm for a whole Christ, in all the parts of His saving office. I'll take Him for my Prophet, and credit [believe] Him in all things; for my Priest, and in Him I'll put all my trust; and for my King, to whom, Thy grace enabling me, I'll yield a sincere, preserving obedience.' This is plainly a renewed covenant.

Second, consider also the actions of eating and drinking, and you'll see further evidence of a covenant transaction. At this holy Supper we come to eat and drink with the blessed God. He spreads a Table, and provides us food so that, eating and drinking, we may receive nourishment for our spiritual life. Now, eating and drinking and feasting together, we may observe in Scripture history, were the usual appendages of compacts or covenants, as we may see in Genesis 26:30 and Genesis 31:44-46, where we find Isaac and Abimelech, Jacob and Laban concluding their compacts with a feast. The eating and drinking together of those who were at variance [dispute] implies an antecedent agreement, for it is a token of friendly familiarity not wont [usually] to be afforded to enemies.

This will be further evident from a third consideration, which is taken from that which we feast upon at the Lord's Table: the memorials of the great Christian sacrifice. It is a solemn feast upon the memorials of the sacrifice of infinite virtue that was offered by our Savior upon the cross for sin. It is easy to observe how commonly covenants between God and man were attended with sacrifices. Thus it was in Noah's case; 'twas the same in Abraham's case (Gen. 8 – 9 and 15). So also sacrifices accompany the covenant God entered into with the Israelites all in a body (Exod. 24:5, 8), and by such sacrifices offered the covenant made was confirmed.

'Gather My saints together unto Me; those that have made a covenant with Me by sacrifice' (Ps. 50:5). To this our blessed Lord seems to allude when, at the institution of the Supper, He says, 'This cup is the new testament in My blood.'

Let us think how strange an instance it is of the condescension by the great Majesty of heaven that He should vouchsafe [grant] to hold any federal communion with such as we are, with us sinners, who have so much provoked Him as to deserve to be utterly abandoned by Him; that God should suffer us to lay hold of His covenant, that He should admit us to feast with Him upon the signs and seals of it, admit us to such a relationship of familiarity, and advance us to such an honor, which is at the same time so much for our benefit, comfort, and security. Oh, bless the Lord and magnify His name!

**Calamy, 24–27, 29–30, 36–37**

### Not for conversion but for covenant communion

We need to realize that the Lord comes to us in the administration of the Lord's Supper. He comes to us in order to complement the message of the gospel, the promises of the covenant of grace, with the signs and seals of this covenant. Thus, our celebration of the Lord's Supper is not in the first place an act whereby we bear witness to our conversion, our pious frame, or our relationship to the Lord — even though these things may also be discussed. Rather, it is primarily God's act towards us, whereas our partaking is the reciprocal act. It is in the Lord's Supper, and thus sacramentally, that the Lord grants us a sign and seal of His love and faithfulness. As a sacrament it is a warranty — a visible sealing of the veracity of His promises. Furthermore, a believing partaking of this sacrament will be subservient to the strengthening of our faith due to the secret operation of the Holy Spirit accompanying the sacrament.

In a sacrament (and thus also applicable to the Lord's Supper) the focus is in the first place on a message which comes from God to us — the message of who and what the triune covenant God is and remains for His people. In order to celebrate it in a godly manner, we must belong to those people who have an experiential need for that promise — who desire to be nourished and confirmed by that sacrament. This necessarily includes that we must possess a 'divine right' to partake of the Lord's Supper.

We should also make a clear distinction between the act of celebrating the Lord's Supper itself and some matters which do not pertain to the essentials of this sacrament and its use, though they are important in and of themselves. For instance, I will mention a few: Some might think the celebration of the Lord's Supper is making confession of their sins; or taking refuge in Jesus' redeeming blood; or a declaration of their love to the Lord, His people and service, etc. Certainly these are blessed things in and of themselves; and they must indeed be present when spiritually partaking of communion. However, they are matters we can also practice apart from the Lord's Supper. They must already exist before we go to the holy Table. All these can already be practiced at home — yes, it should already have been practiced there.

What then is the Lord's Supper? Well, the sacrament directs us to the perfect sacrifice of Christ on the cross as the only ground and foundation of our salvation. What then is the difference between being in a spiritual frame on my knees in my closet, or being at the Lord's Supper? As a sacrament, the

Lord's Supper signifies to us the foundation of our salvation
in a distinct and special way; namely, by way of the signs of
broken bread and poured out wine. We should bear in mind,
however, that these signs are also held forth to us as a seal.
And what does that mean? Well, the promise of God in Christ
Jesus is of such extraordinary magnitude that it seems almost
impossible to apply also to such a one as I am. Therefore the
Lord, by means of His Supper, stamps the seal of confirmation
upon this promise. We receive no additional promise — the
sacrament simply seals the promise fully given of God to us.

It is as though the Lord says, 'Have you put your trust in
Christ's righteousness in the way of true repentance? Then
receive here the visible and tangible pledge that you can truly
and completely depend on My grace and faithfulness!' God,
so to speak, places the ring of spiritual betrothal on our finger.
We did already taste pardoning love at home — the Lord's
Supper puts God's seal on it.

**Wisse, 100–101**

## Joined to God in covenant bonds

Now the covenant bindeth mutually. God bindeth Himself
to give grace to us, and we bind ourselves to live unto God:
Exodus 24:6-8: 'And Moses took half of the blood, and put it
in basons; and half of the blood he sprinkled on the altar. And
he took the book of the covenant, and read in the audience
of the people: and they said, All that the LORD hath said will
we do, and be obedient. And Moses took the blood, and
sprinkled it on the people, and said, Behold the blood of the

covenant, which the LORD hath made with you concerning all these words.'

Well, then, sacraments on God's part are signs and seals of the promise of grace; on our part, an obligation to obedience. God bindeth Himself to be our God, and we bind ourselves to be His people. God to be our God, that is to be a benefactor becoming an infinite and eternal power; that is, the meaning of 'I will be your God' (Matt. 22:32; Heb. 11:16); that is, Father, Son, and Holy Ghost, will employ all His wisdom, power, and goodness to keep us from all evil, and bestow on us all good: Genesis 15:1: 'Fear not, Abraham; I am thy shield, and thy exceeding great reward'; and Psalm 84:11: 'For the LORD God is a sun and shield; the LORD will give grace and glory: no good thing will he withhold from them that walk uprightly.' Here a shield, hereafter a reward; both in part here, both fully hereafter, when the sun is in his meridian [at noon]. Again, on the other side, we bind ourselves to be His people; that is, as to entrance and progress. As to entrance, Acts 20:21: 'Testifying both to the Jews, and also to the Greeks, repentance toward God, and faith toward our Lord Jesus Christ.' So it is an obligation to repentance and faith; this is making the covenant. As to progress, continuance, and keeping covenant; so we bind ourselves to new obedience: Hebrews 5:9: 'He became the author of eternal salvation unto all them that obey him.'

Now, then, if we come aright, we must come with a true heart, and in full assurance of faith (Heb. 10:22). With an assurance of faith, that God will be as good as His word, pardoning, sanctifying, blessing, and that He will keep us to everlasting glory; and with a true heart bind ourselves to a return to our duty, depending on the Redeemer's sacrifice, and to walk in all new obedience.

**Manton, 15:493–94**

### Tasting God's goodness in the seal of the covenant

Divine goodness is eminent in the sacraments He hath affixed to this covenant, especially in the Lord's Supper. As He gave Himself in His Son, so He gives His Son in the sacrament; He doth not only give Him as a sacrifice upon the cross for the expiation of our crimes, but as a feast upon the Table for the nourishment of our souls. In the one He was given to be offered, in this He gives Him to be partaked of, with all the fruits of his death; under the image of the sacramental signs, every believer doth eat the flesh and drink the blood of the great Mediator of the covenant. The words of Christ, Matthew 26:26, 28: 'This is my body,' and 'This is my blood,' are true to the end of the world. This is the most delicious viand [food] of heaven, the most exquisite dainty food God can feed us with; the delight of the Deity, the admiration of angels. A feast with God is great, but a feast on God is greater.

Under those signs that body is presented; that which was conceived by the Spirit, inhabited by the Godhead, bruised by the Father to be our food, as well as our propitiation, is presented to us on the Table. That blood which satisfied justice, washed away our guilt on the cross, and pleads for our persons at the throne of grace; that blood which silenced the curse, pacified heaven, and purged earth, is given to us for our refreshment. This is the bread sent from heaven, the true manna; the cup is the 'cup of blessing', and therefore a cup of goodness (1 Cor. 10:16). It is true, bread doth not cease to be bread, nor the wine cease to be wine; neither of them lose their substance, but both acquire a sanctification by the relation they have to that which they represent, and give a nourishment to that faith that receives them.

His goodness is seen in the end of it, which is a sealing of the covenant of grace. The common nature and end of sacraments is to seal the covenant they belong to, and the truths of the promises of it. The legal sacraments of circumcision and the Passover sealed the legal promises and the covenant in the Judaical [Jewish] administration of it; and the evangelical sacraments seal the evangelical promises, as a ring confirms the contract of marriage and a seal the articles of a compact; by the same reason circumcision is called a 'seal of the righteousness of the faith' (Rom. 4:11). Other sacraments may have the same title; God doth attest that he will remain firm in His promise, and the receiver attests he will remain firm in his faith.

In all reciprocal covenants there are mutual engagements, and that which serves for a seal on the part of the one, serves for a seal also on the part of the other; God obligeth himself to the performance of the promise, and man engageth himself to the performance of his duty. The thing confirmed by this sacrament is the perpetuity of this covenant in the blood of Christ; whence it is called 'the new testament', or covenant 'in the blood of Christ' (Luke 22:20). In every repetition of it, God, by presenting, confirms His resolution to us of sticking to this covenant for the merit of Christ's blood; and the receiver, by eating the body and drinking the blood, engageth himself to keep close to the condition of faith, expecting a full salvation and a blessed immortality upon the merit of the same blood alone. This sacrament could not be called the new testament or covenant if it had not some relation to the covenant; and what it can be but this I do not understand. The covenant itself was confirmed by the death of Christ (Heb. 9:15), and thereby made unchangeable both in the benefits to us and the condition required of us; but He seals it to our sense in a sacrament to give us strong consolation.

**Charnock, 2:341–43**

## Rejoicing that the all-sufficient God is mine

Here we must be delighting in God, and solacing [comforting] ourselves in His favour. — If we had not a Christ to hope in, being guilty and corrupt, we could not have a God to rejoice in; but, having an Advocate with the Father, so good a plea as Christ dying, and so good a Pleader as Christ interceding, we may not only 'come boldly to the throne of grace, but may sit down under the shadow of it with delight, and behold the beauty of the Lord'. That God who is love, and the God of love, here shows us His 'marvelous loving-kindness; causeth His goodness to pass before us; proclaims His name gracious and merciful'. Here He gives us His love, and thereby invites us to give Him ours. It is a love-feast, the love of Christ is here commemorated, the love of God here offered.

Let it be a pleasure to thee to think, 'that there is a God, and that He is such a one as he hath revealed himself to be'. The being and attributes of God are a terror to those that are unjustified and unsanctified; nothing can be more so: they are willing to believe 'there is no God, or that he is altogether such a one as themselves', because they heartily wish there were none, or one that they could be at peace with, and yet continue their league with sin: but to those who, through grace, partake of a divine nature themselves, nothing is more agreeable, nothing more acceptable, than the thoughts of God's nature and infinite perfections. Delight thyself, therefore, in thinking that there is an infinite and eternal Spirit, who is self-existent and self-sufficient, the best of beings, and the first of causes; the highest of powers, and the richest and kindest of friends and benefactors; the fountain of being and fountain of bliss; the 'Father of lights, the Father of mercies'. Love to think of Him whom thou canst not see, and yet canst not but know; who is not far from thee, and yet between thee and Him there is an infinite, awful distance. Let these thoughts be thy nourishment and refreshment.

Let it be a pleasure to thee to think of 'the obligations thou liest under to this God as the Creator'. He that is the former of my body, and the Father of my spirit, in whom I live, and move, and have my being, is upon that account my rightful owner, my sovereign ruler, whom I am bound to serve. Because He made me, and not I myself, therefore I am not mine own, but His. Please thyself, my soul, with this thought, that thou art not thine own, but His that made thee; nor left to thine own will, but bound up to His; not made for thyself, but designed to be to Him for a name and a praise.

Let it be a pleasure to thee 'to think of the covenant relations wherein this God stands to thee in Jesus Christ'. This is especially to be our delight in this sealing ordinance: though the sacrament directs us immediately to Christ, yet through Him it leads us to the Father. He died, 'the just for the unjust, that he might bring us to God' [1 Peter 3:18]. To God therefore we must go as our end and rest, by Christ as our way; to God as a Father, by Christ as Mediator. Come, then, my soul, and see with joy and the highest satisfaction, the God that made thee entering into covenant with thee, and engaging to make thee happy. Hear him saying to thee, my soul, 'I am thy salvation, thy shield', and not only thy bountiful rewarder, but 'thine exceeding great reward'; I am and will be to thee a God all-sufficient; a God that is enough. 'Fear thou not, for I am with thee', wherever thou art; 'be not dismayed, for I am thy God'; whatever thou wantest, whatever thou losest, call me God, even thine own God. When thou art weak, I will strengthen thee, yea, when thou art helpless, I will help thee; yea, when thou art ready to sink, 'I will uphold thee with the right hand of my righteousness.' The God that cannot lie has said it, and here seals it to thee, 'I will never leave thee nor forsake thee.' Let this be to thee, my soul, the voice of joy and gladness, making even broken bones to rejoice. Encourage thyself in the Lord thy God. He is thy Shepherd, thou shalt not want anything that is good for thee. 'Thy Maker is thy husband, the Lord of hosts is his name'; and as the bridegroom rejoices over the bride, so shall thy God rejoice over thee. He shall rest in His love to thee: rest then in thy love to Him, and rejoice in Him always. The Lord is thy lawgiver, thy King that will save thee: swear allegiance to him, then, with gladness and loud hosannas. 'Let Israel rejoice in him that made him (that new-made him); let the children of Zion be joyful in their King.' What wouldst thou more? This God is thy God for ever and ever.

**Henry, *Communicant's Companion*, 208–211**

# 9

# FEEDING ON CHRIST BY FAITH

*Be not carried about with divers and strange doctrines. For it
is a good thing that the heart be established with grace; not
with meats, which have not profited them that have been
occupied therein. We have an altar, whereof they have no
right to eat which serve the tabernacle*
(Hebrews 13:9-10).

## A rich means of grace

Here, then, is the singular consolation which we derive
from the Supper. It directs and leads us to the cross
of Jesus Christ and to His resurrection, to certify us that
whatever iniquity there may be in us, the Lord nevertheless
recognizes and accepts us as righteous — whatever materials
of death may be in us, He nevertheless gives us life — whatever
misery may be in us, He nevertheless fills us with all felicity.
Or to explain the matter more simply — as in ourselves we are
devoid of all good, and have not one particle of what might

help to procure salvation, the Supper is an attestation that, having been made partakers of the death and passion of Jesus Christ, we have everything that is useful and salutary to us.

The second benefit of the Supper is, that it admonishes and incites us more strongly to recognize the blessings which we have received, and receive daily from the Lord Jesus, in order that we may ascribe to Him the praise which is due. For in ourselves we are so negligent that we rarely think of the goodness of God, if He do not arouse us from our indolence [laziness], and urge us to our duty. Now there cannot be a spur which can pierce us more to the quick than when He makes us, so to speak, see with the eye, touch with the hand, and distinctly perceive this inestimable blessing of feeding on His own substance. This He means to intimate when He commands us to show forth His death till He come (1 Cor. 11:26). If it is then so essential to salvation not to overlook the gifts which God has given us, but diligently to keep them in mind, and extol them to others for mutual edification; we see another singular advantage of the Supper in this, that it draws us off from ingratitude, and allows us not to forget the benefit which our Lord Jesus bestowed upon us in dying for us, but induces us to render Him thanks, and, as it were, publicly protest how much we are indebted to Him.

The third advantage of the sacrament consists in furnishing a most powerful incitement to live holily, and especially observe charity and brotherly love toward all. For seeing we have been made members of Jesus Christ, being incorporated into Him, and united with Him as our head, it is most reasonable that we should become conformable to Him in purity and innocence, and especially that we should cultivate charity and concord together as becomes members of the same body. But to understand this advantage properly, we must not suppose that our Lord warns, incites, and inflames our hearts by the external sign merely; for the principal point is, that He operates in us inwardly by His Holy Spirit, in order to give efficacy to His ordinance, which He has destined for that purpose, as an instrument by which He wishes to do His work in us. Wherefore, inasmuch as the virtue of the Holy Spirit is conjoined with the sacraments when we duly receive them, we have reason to hope they will prove a good mean and aid to make us grow and advance in holiness of life, and specially in charity.

**Calvin, 168, 173–74**

## Strengthening faith and repentance

When we behold the bread broken, and the wine poured out, we are thereby to be put in mind, that the body of Christ was crucified, and His blood shed for our sins. That His blessed body was broken and torn with stripes and wounds, with whips, nails, and spear, His blood, yea, even His heart blood poured out, and His holy soul pressed and pained with the heavy burden of His Father's displeasure for our iniquities (Isa. 53:5). And to this end our Savior instituted this His Last Supper, not that we should rest in itself, and (as it were) the deed done, or in the outward rites and actions; but that it might put us in remembrance of His death, and sufferings, and of the great benefit of our redemption wrought by them. For God is not chiefly worshipped by our eyes, ears, hands, and taste, or with outward ceremonies and observations; but in spirit and truth. And therefore let us not rest in outward words and ceremonies, but chiefly set on work our hearts and affections, and bring all we do unto an holy and spiritual use.

And the consideration of Christ's death represented by the breaking of bread, and pouring out of the wine, serveth to exercise and renew our unfeigned [sincere] repentance: as first, to work in us an hearty sorrow for our sins, because by them we have crucified the Lord of life, and put Him to death, that came to save us, even when as we were strangers and enemies (Zech. 12:10). For Judas that betrayed Him, the priests and Pharisees that accused Him, Pilate that condemned Him, the soldiers that whipped Him, nailed Him to the cross, and pierced His side with a spear, were but our executioners to inflict on him those punishments which our sin deserved, and God's justice imposed. And therefore let us beat our hearts for sorrow, that we have caused life itself to be put unto a shameful death, Him to be condemned that came to justify and save us, and for a time to be held under the bondage of death, who came to redeem and deliver us from death, and out of thralldom [slavery] of all our spiritual enemies, and purchase for us eternal life and blessedness.

The consideration hereof should work our hearts to a true hatred of sin, as the greatest evil, and to a serious resolution and endeavor, to leave and forsake it for the time to come. For how should that be any more pleasing unto us, which was so displeasing and odious unto God, that He punished it so severely in His only begotten and best beloved Son? How should it seem light unto us which did lie upon Him as an intolerable burden, pressing out of His innocent body that sweat of water and blood? How shall that be any more sweet unto us, that made him drink gall and vinegar, yea, that which was much more bitter, the dregs of God's wrath, and the cup of His heavy displeasure, even to the bottom? How should not this make us so to abhor all sin, that we would not for all the world wittingly, and willingly fall into it, lest we should again crucify the Son of God, and make a mock of Him (Heb. 6:6)?

And as the temperance of Christ's death and bitter passion serveth as a powerful means to renew and increase our repentance, it is alike effectual to strengthen our faith against all the assaults and fiery darts of Satan. For though our spiritual enemies be many and mighty, yet our Savior by His death hath overcome and triumphed over them upon His cross: though our sins be heinous and grievous, yet if we repent and believe, they shall not separate us from the love of God, seeing Christ's death is a propitiatory sacrifice, whereby God's justice is satisfied, and His wrath appeased. As therefore we cast our eye upon our sins to humble us under their burden, and bring us to repentance; so we are to cast the other upon our Savior Christ hanging upon the cross, who having taken all our burden upon Himself, doth now invite us to come unto Him, that we may be saved.

**Downame, 204–207**

### Weakening sin, strengthening spiritual life

The benefits of this ordinance are many.

(1) *Weakening of sin*; not physically but morally [that is, by influencing our thoughts and consciences]. The lively

representation and consideration of the death of Christ, with all its circumstances, is a strong incentive and assistance to the mortifying [of] sin in us; and there is no branch of the body of death, but some consideration or other fetched from the death of Christ, hath a virtue to destroy. How can any be proud when he sees Christ lay down His life in the form of a mean [lowly] man; how can he be covetous, when he sees Christ turning His back upon the profits of the world? Christ upon the cross, viewed by a sparkling eye of faith, would work the same effect in our souls, which the looking upon the serpent in the wilderness wrought in the Israelites' poisoned bodies, expelling the venom from the vitals and out-works of the members, and abating the fury of a corrupt paroxysm [acute illness].

Now as feathered arrows will fly further, and pierce deeper, than when they are carried by their own weight only, so such considerations, when helped by sensible representations, do more excite the faculty to a vigorous operation by a more sensible affecting the mind. The Word declares the evil of sin, and the sacrament shows it in the person of our Saviour; sin is known by the Word to be deadly, and it is seen to be so in the Supper. Then is the soul most affected against sin, when God's indignation against it is manifested, when it beholds Christ made a curse, and bearing all that the law denounceth against sin, and sees the desert of sin and the terrors of wrath. Never doth sin look so ghastly, and repentance so sorrowfully, as when Christ and the soul meet together in this ordinance.

As Christ upon the cross expiated sin, so Christ in the Supper mortifies sin by His Spirit, and purgeth those iniquities which are as a veil between the face of God and the joy of our souls.

(2) *Nourishment of the soul*. In regard of the insensible decay of the spirits of the body, there is need of a continual supply to recruit [restore] them, and keep them up in their due vigour; our souls stand in no less need of being succoured by a feast of fat things full of marrow. The flesh hath its provisions, and grace must have hers. In the nourishment of the body, the meat, by the vital heat in the stomach, is turned into the substance of the body; so by a believing participation of Christ in the sacrament, we are turned into the image of Christ, and nourished up by it to eternal life. His flesh is meat indeed, and His blood is drink indeed (John 6:55).

He is given to us as nourishment: 'Take, eat, This is my body,' as nourishment to be incorporated with us; the bread is the sign of His body, and His body is the bread of the soul; the element conveys vigour to the body, and the thing signified strength to the soul, and recruits it with new spirits. What bread and wine do physically convey to the body, which is strength, comfort, nourishment, that doth the body and blood of Christ by faith convey to the soul, quickening, comforting, strengthening, cherishing grace.

**Charnock, 4:408–409**

## One bread, one body, one church

The Lord's Supper is well fitted to cement the bonds of Christian brotherhood.

Christians, all true believers, are one body, the mystical body of Christ — that body of which He is the Head; and the strongest affection and sympathy ought, of course, to exist, and prevail among them. This, however, will materially depend, as to its reality and experience, not merely on the fact that they are one body, but on the conviction and feeling of that fact; just as the members of the natural body sympathize one with another, not merely because they are members of the same body, but rather because they feel that they are.

Now the Lord's Supper, beyond any other ordinance, brings this fact to the observation, and experience of Christians. It is, to begin with, designed exclusively for Christians; and is supposed, therefore, to be exclusively attended by them. It is an occasion, and the only one, when, on scriptural principles, they are supposed to appear, as a body visibly, and manifestly separated from the rest of mankind. It is an occasion, therefore, when the believer is necessarily, and most pointedly, reminded of the existence of that body, and of the brotherhood it involves; and not only so, but when also, by reason of the nature and circumstances of the rite itself, the peculiar characteristics of that body, in which its brotherhood actually consists — namely, the equality, relationship, and oneness or identity of nature, of all its members — are prominently brought to view; these very particulars being most strikingly, and significantly set forth, and exhibited at the Lord's Supper.

Their equality, for instance — how plainly is this recognized in the fact that no respect of persons, no distinction of any kind whatever, in reference to communicants, is there allowed to be countenanced or observed; the rich and the poor, the high and the low, the mighty and the mean, the educated and the ignorant, all alike meet, and are mingled together undistinguished, they are, in short, regarded simply and exclusively as members of Christ, and as such treated; all else is forgotten, lost sight of — all natural, or circumstantial, differences are merged in that, which is spiritually common — the most perfect equality is, as a fact, strictly maintained.

So in regard to relationship — this is exhibited and maintained at the Lord's Supper, in the fact that all partake not only together of the same food, but also at the same Table. Communicants assemble at the same Table. But that Table is spread for God's children alone, none others are invited to be guests, or have right there; therefore all who are found there, all who are guests, and assemble at that Table, must (unless good cause be shown to the contrary) be supposed to be children. Communicants are bound, therefore, so to regard each other, each one must look upon the rest as members with himself of the household of God, and of the family of heaven; and thus the relationship of believers, their brotherhood, is at the Lord's Table not only signally declared, but its recognition also necessarily required of all who attend.

The same may be shown in regard to the oneness, or identity of nature, that exists among them, and so to the reality of the union which knits, and ties, the body together. This is exhibited, and shown forth, as the apostle maintains, by the fact of their eating the same bread — 'For we being many are one bread and one body: for we are all partakers of that one bread' (1 Cor. 10:17); that is, according to the apostles' argument, since all who partake, partake of one and the same bread, therefore all, who partake, constitute one, and the same body.

**Molyneux, 38–41**

## Anticipating the kingdom feast

The Lord's Table around which we gather as Christians from time to time is, as we have seen, first of all, a place at which we remember Him. It is also the sign of God's pledge; God's covenant to us in the precious blood of Christ. The Lord's Table is also the centre of our spiritual fellowship one with another in Christ. But I want us to think of the Lord's Supper now as the service of hope.

There is something forward-looking in the Lord's Supper, and it is this hope that I want you to catch. Have you ever said goodbye to somebody with the sinking feeling in your heart that you would never see them again? But if there has been the faintest hope that you would see them once more, that there would be some opportunity of being reunited, well, what a difference that has made! The Lord left His disciples and He went up where He was before. But His going away was not the end of hope, it was not the beginning of depression: because concerning Him there was not merely the faint hope, but the clearest teaching that He would come again. The Lord's Supper, looking not only backwards to the cross, but also forward to the second coming of the Lord Jesus Christ, is the token and constant witness to the fact that the Lord Jesus is to return and that before us there stretches out a vast prospect of glorious hope. The Lord's Supper is the token of the Lord's return.

Look now at the First Epistle to the Corinthians, for example, in chapter 11. At the end of the words which describe the institution of this Supper, we have words like these: 'For as often as ye eat this bread, and drink this cup, ye do show the Lord's death till he come.' 'Till He come.' The Lord's Supper every time says to us, 'He is coming back.' This not a perpetual observance.

There is to come a glorious moment when it will be consummated and realized in glory that is unspeakable, in an intimacy of face-to-face union with God which we have never imagined down here. It is to be observed 'till He come'. The Lord's Supper, then, is a service of hope.

Not only is this hope clearly stated in words like these in Paul's letter, but there are features about the institution of the Lord's Supper which build up to this great expectation. Turn to the words of Matthew 26:29. The previous verses describe the institution of this service, and then our Lord says, 'But I say unto you, I will not drink henceforth of this fruit of the vine, until that day when I drink it new with you in my Father's kingdom.'

Listen once more to what our Lord says to His disciples in Luke 22:29-30: 'And I appoint unto you a kingdom, as my Father hath appointed unto me; that ye may eat and drink at my table in my kingdom.' The last passage to which I would like you to turn is in the last book of the Bible (Rev. 19:9). 'And he saith unto me, Write, Blessed are they which are called unto the marriage supper of the Lamb.' Thus, when our Lord chose in His sovereignty to keep His disciples reminded of Him by the institution of a feast, He was building not only on the past, that is to say, the Passover feast; He was also building on the expectation that was in every godly Jewish heart that

Messiah's glory and His vindication would be expressed in the form of a wondrous banquet.

The Lord's Supper is, therefore, anticipatory: it points beyond itself to something bigger than itself. In fact, the Lord's Supper is always saying, 'Till He come'; 'Till He come'.

**Kevan, 71–72, 74**

# 10

# PRAYERS OF COMMUNION

*What shall I render unto the LORD for all his benefits*
*toward me?*
*I will take the cup of salvation, and call upon*
*the name of the LORD*
(Psalm 116:12-13).

## Let Christ's flesh be meat indeed to us

Lord, now we are invited to come eat of wisdom's bread, and drink of the wine that she has mingled (Prov. 9:5), give us to hunger and thirst after righteousness (Matt. 5:6): And being called to the marriage supper of the Lamb (Rev. 19:9), give us the wedding garment (Matt. 22:11).

Awake, O north wind, and come thou south, and blow upon our garden, that the spices thereof may flow forth; and then let our Beloved come into His garden, and eat His pleasant fruits (Cant. 4:16).

Draw us, and we will run after Thee; bring us into Thy chambers, that there we may be glad and rejoice in Thee, and may remember Thy love more than wine. And when the King sits at His Table, let our spikenard send forth the smell thereof (Cant. 1:12).

And the good Lord pardon every one that prepareth his heart to seek God, the LORD God of his fathers, though he be not cleansed according to the purification of the sanctuary. Hear our prayers, and heal the people (2 Chron. 30:18-20).

O let this cup of blessing which we bless, be the communion of the blood of Christ (1 Cor. 10:16), let this bread which we break, be the communion of the body of Christ, and enable us herein to show the Lord's death till He come (1 Cor. 11:26).

Now let us be joined to the Lord in an everlasting covenant (Jer. 50:5), so joined to the Lord, as to become one spirit with Him (1 Cor. 6:17). Now let us be made partakers of Christ, by holding fast the beginning of our confidence steadfast unto the end (Heb. 3:14).

Let Christ's flesh be meat indeed to us, and His blood drink indeed: and give us so by faith to eat His flesh, and drink His blood, that He may dwell in us, and we in Him, and we may live by Him (John 6:55-57).

Let the cross of Christ, which is to the Jews a stumbling block, and to the Greeks foolishness, be to us the wisdom of God, and the power of God (1 Cor. 1:23-24).

Seal to us the remission of sins, the gift of the Holy Ghost
(Acts 2:38), and the promise of eternal life (1 John 2:25), and
enable us to take this cup of salvation, and to call on the name
of the Lord (Ps. 116:13).

**Henry, *Method for Prayer*, 164–65**

### Enliven my faith to apprehend the Saviour

God of all good,
I bless Thee for the means of grace;
    teach me to see in them Thy loving purposes
    and the joy and strength of my soul.
Thou hast prepared for me a feast;
and though I am unworthy to sit down as guest,
I wholly rest on the merits of Jesus,
    and hide myself beneath His righteousness;
When I hear His tender invitation
    and see His wondrous grace,
    I cannot hesitate, but must come to Thee in love.
By Thy Spirit enliven my faith rightly to discern
    and spiritually to apprehend the Saviour.
While I gaze upon the emblems of my Saviour's death,
    may I ponder why He died, and hear Him say,
        'I gave My life to purchase yours,
        presented Myself an offering to expiate your sin,
        shed My blood to blot out your guilt,
        opened My side to make you clean,
        endured your curses to set you free,
        bore your condemnation to satisfy divine justice.'
O may I rightly grasp the breadth and length of this design,
draw near, obey, extend the hand, take the bread,

> receive the cup, eat and drink,
> testify before all men that I do for myself,
> gladly, in faith, reverence and love, receive my Lord,
> to be my life, strength, nourishment, joy, delight.

In the Supper I remember His eternal love, boundless grace,
> infinite compassion, agony, cross, redemption,
> and receive assurance of pardon, adoption, life, glory.

As the outward elements nourish my body,
> so may Thy indwelling Spirit invigorate my soul,
> until that day when I hunger and thirst no more,
> and sit with Jesus at His heavenly feast.

**Bennet, ed., 197**

## Let me embrace My Prophet, Priest, and King

O Lord my God, who art in Thyself infinite in all goodness, and most gracious to all that seek Thee in Thy holy ordinances with sincere and upright hearts; who performest all Thy promises, and keepest covenant for ever with all those that fear and serve Thee. I humbly acknowledge that I am utterly unworthy to approach into Thy glorious presence, who art so full of majesty, that even Thy holy angels do cover their faces when Thou appearest. Yet seeing Thou of Thy mere grace hast invited me this day to come as a guest to Thy Table; I beseech Thee (good Lord) to assist me with Thy grace and Holy Spirit, that I may come prepared, as becometh such a presence at such a banquet.

Unclothe me (dear God) of all the polluted rags of my sinful corruptions, and adorn me with the wedding-garment, put on by a lively faith, even the rich robe of Christ's righteousness, and with all sanctifying and saving graces which are required in all those who will come as worthy guests to this holy Table. Especially work in me a hunger and thirst after this spiritual food, and being humbled in the sight and sense of my own emptiness, let me earnestly desire above all things to be made partaker of this bread of life which came down from heaven, of which whosoever eateth shall live for ever. And seeing Thou art an Holy Spirit infinite in all excellencies and perfections, give me grace to perform this holy service unto Thee, suitably and agreeably to Thine own nature, not in a cold and formal manner with the outward man alone, but also with heart and soul, in Spirit and Truth.

O Lord my God, Thou in Thine infinite mercy and love hast sent Thine only and dear Son into the world to redeem me out of all my misery, when as I was dead in trespasses and sins, and the child of wrath as well as others. And when I was not only a stranger but also an enemy, Thou hast given Him to be my Mediator by whom I might be reconciled unto Thee. The which great work He hath accomplished in His threefold office, as being a Prophet who hath revealed Thy will unto me; a Priest to offer Himself in an all-sufficient sacrifice for sin, and for satisfying of Thy justice and appeasing of Thy wrath, and to make intercession for me at Thy right hand; and a King to rule and govern me, preserve and protect me from all mine enemies.

O Lord Thy holy name be blessed and praised for this inestimable gift of Thy Son. Let me (O Lord) receive Him by a lively faith, and rest wholly upon Him as an all-sufficient

Mediator. Let me acknowledge Him mine only Prophet to teach me, receiving His doctrine as the only truth, and rejecting all other which differeth from it; mine only Priest resting upon His all-sufficient sacrifice once offered for sin to satisfy Thy justice; and upon His intercession only, seeing there is no other Mediator in heaven or earth but He alone. Finally, let me acknowledge Him as mine only King for preservation and protection, and in all things submit myself to be directed, ruled and governed by the scepter of His Word and Holy Spirit, not suffering sin or Satan to reign in me as in time past, seeing Christ my King hath redeemed me out of their thralldom [or slavery] to do Him service.

**Downname, 287–89**

## Blessed be the Father of Christ, the Father of mercies

O Father of mercy, and God of all consolation, seeing all creatures do acknowledge and confess Thee to be their Governor and Lord, it becometh us the workmanship of Thine own hands, to reverence and magnify Thy godly majesty.

First, for that Thou hast created us to Thine own image and similitude: but chiefly because Thou hast delivered us from the everlasting death and damnation, into the which Satan drew mankind by the means of sin, from the bondage whereof, neither man nor angel was able to make us free. But Thou, O Lord, rich in mercy, and infinite in goodness, hast provided our redemption to stand in Thine only and most beloved Son, whom of very love Thou didst give to be made man like unto us in all things, sin excepted: that in His body He might receive the punishment of our transgression, by His death to make satisfaction to Thy justice, and by His resurrection, to destroy Him that was the author of death, and so to bring again life to the world, from which the whole offspring of Adam was most justly exiled.

O Lord, we acknowledge that no creature was able to comprehend the length and breadth, the deepness and height, of that Thy most excellent love which moved Thee to show mercy where none was deserved: to promise and give life, where death had gotten victory: to receive us into Thy grace, when we could do nothing but rebel against Thy majesty.

O Lord, the blind dullness of our corrupt nature will not suffer us sufficiently to weigh these Thy most ample benefits. Yet nevertheless at the commandment of Jesus Christ our Lord, we present ourselves to this His Table (which He hath left to be used in remembrance of His death until His coming again) to declare and witness before the world, that by Him alone we have received liberty and life: that by Him alone Thou dost acknowledge us to be Thy children and heirs: that by Him alone we have entrance to the throne of Thy grace: that by Him alone we are possessed in our spiritual kingdom, to eat and drink at His Table: with whom we have our conversation presently in heaven: and by whom our bodies shall be raised up again from the dust, and shall be placed with Him in that endless joy, which Thou, O Father of mercy, hast prepared for Thine elect before the foundation of the world was laid.

And these most inestimable benefits we acknowledge and confess to have received of Thy free mercy and grace, by Thine only beloved Son Jesus Christ, for the which therefore we Thy congregation, moved by Thy Holy Spirit, render to Thee all thanks, praise, and glory, forever, and ever, Amen.

**Day, 89–91**

## Pleas and praises to the merciful Saviour

Dear Saviour of my soul, look upon the sinner Thou hast redeemed with Thy most precious blood. I come because Thou hast bidden me, and my soul needeth the refreshment Thou hast provided. Never do I draw near, but I bring with me fresh cause of humiliation, and carry new burdens to Thee, my Lord, from which I need relief. Look upon me in Thy wonted [usual] compassion, and pity and pardon all the faithlessness with which I stand chargeable before Thee. Jesus, my hope is in Thee. Ten thousand times have I forfeited all the mercies of my God, but Thou hast been my Advocate, Thy blood hath spoken for me; still, Lord, let it speak, and sprinkled on me, purge my heart from dead works to serve the living God.

When now again I am drawing near to Thee, draw near to my sinful soul. Strengthen my confidence in Thy love, when I partake of the instituted pledges Thou hast left me. O comfort me with the assurance that Thou art mine. Teach these eyes with tears of penitence and joy to look upon Thy broken body; give me thus that repentance unto salvation never to be repented of. O, my Lord, conquered by Thy dying love, may every lust be offered up a willing sacrifice at Thy cross; take them, Lord, slay them before Thee; consume the dross of base affections, purify my soul, and with this sacred fire refine it like Thine own.

Anointed Jesus, save me from every sin; set up within my soul
Thy kingdom of righteousness, and peace and joy in the Holy
Ghost; reign over a willing subject, and let Thy service be ever
the happy freedom of my soul. Thou askest nothing from me
which it is not my happiness to renounce; Thou commandest
nothing wherein it is not my happiness to obey Thee.

Thou knowest, Lord, my simpleness [or foolishness], and my
faults are not hid from Thee; Thou knowest it is the desire of
my soul to love and please Thee; it is my bitterness that I ever
offend Thee: O when shall I have done with sin? When shall
I grieve no more Thy Spirit in me? O Lord, when shall it yet
be? Continue to be gracious; draw me nearer to Thy blessed
self, that I may run more eagerly after Thee; show me more
of Thy beauty, that sin may grow more hateful in my eyes;
lay Thy hand upon me, and fashion me; O fashion me, dear
Redeemer, in Thy own blessed image, and make me wholly
such as Thou wouldst have me to be.

Receive my thanks, dear suffering Saviour, Thou
compassionate High-priest, who canst be touched with the
feeling of Thy people's infirmities, blessing and praise be
ever Thine. Help me daily to be telling of Thy salvation, till
Thou shalt give me a place with those blessed spirits of the
just made perfect, whose happy labour is everlasting songs of
thanksgiving to Thee, who was slain, and hast redeemed us
to God by Thy blood, and made us kings and priests, that we
might reign with Thee in Thy kingdom for ever. Amen.

**Haweis, 135–39**

# PART III
# GIVING THANKS AND
# GOING ON WITH CHRIST

# 11

# GRATITUDE FOR THE SIGN, THE SON, AND THE SPIRIT

*My God, my God, why hast thou forsaken me?... The meek
shall eat and be satisfied: they shall praise the LORD that seek
him: your heart shall live for ever. All the ends of the world
shall remember and turn unto the LORD: and all the kindreds
of the nations shall worship before thee*
(Psalm 22:1, 26-27).

### Amazed, grateful, and rejoicing in God

Q What should be a matter of admiration to us when we
come from the Lord's Table?

A. We should wonder at the goodness and condescension
of God to us, that He should have had such thoughts of love
for us, provided such a Surety and sacrifice for us as His own
beloved Son, entertained us at His Table, taken into covenant
and communion with Himself, and given us guarantees of
our everlasting inheritance; and that He who is higher than

the heavens should have done all this for creatures who are by nature mean [low or despicable] as worms, nay, polluted and loathsome in the sight of God (Ps. 8:4; 113:5-6; 2 Chron. 6:18; 2 Sam. 7:18).

Q. What is it that we should be thankful for when we come from the Lord's Table?

A. We should be thankful to God for His love in giving Christ, for Christ's love in giving Himself, and for the love of the Holy Spirit in revealing Christ to us and in us. Also, we should bless God for all the blessed fruits of this love, particularly for the well-ordered covenant of grace and the seals of it; for pardon of sin, and for all the rich benefits sealed to us at a communion Table; that we live in a Goshen on earth and have the prospect of a Canaan above (Luke 2:14; Eph. 1:3; 2 Cor. 9:12, 15; Rev. 1:5; Deut. 8:10).

Q. What is it that we should rejoice in when we go from the Lord's Table?

A. 1. In the persons of the glorious Trinity: in God the Father as our covenanted God and portion, in God the Son as our Savior and Redeemer, and in God the Holy Spirit as our Comforter and Sanctifier (Ps. 43:4; Rom. 5:11).

A. 2. In the attributes and perfections of God, particularly in His goodness, mercy, wisdom, might, immutability, and faithfulness, as being all in confederacy with us and engaged to promote our well-being and happiness (Ps. 104:24; 73:25-26; 48:14; Hab. 3:17-18).

A. 3. We ought to rejoice in our Redeemer's love, His wonderful undertaking, and the glorious victories and purchase He has obtained for us (Phil. 3:5; Luke 1:46-51).

A. 4. We should rejoice in the ways of God, having our hearts lifted up in them and enlarged both to run and to sing in the ways of the Lord, and to go about every commanded duty with pleasure (Acts 8:39; 2 Chron. 17:6; Ps. 119:32; 138:5).

**Willison, *Sacramental Catechism*, 265–67**

### Highest love, stooping to the weakest

Behold, hearers, what manner of kindness the Lord shows to His church, when He bestows this Supper on her. Is it not a great favour, that He surrenders Himself for vile sinners, to take away their sins once for all, that they may be forgiven? That He suffers His body to be broken, His blood to be shed? That He endures such grievous sufferings and pains, inflicted on Him by wicked men, by angels, yea, even by His Father? What an ardent love must have been kindled in His soul, when He died for you, O believers, while ye were yet sinners and ungodly! Are ye able to comprehend, is it in your power to conceive the breadth, and the length, the depth and the height of the love of Christ, that He gives you His flesh to eat and His blood to drink?

It was a privilege of Israel that they might eat of their thank-offerings with joy (Deut. 27:7), but they might not eat of their sacrifices of atonement, although they were only irrational animals; what a precious privilege is it then, that ye may eat of the flesh of the Son of God, which was broken, and His blood, which was shed for atonement, as an evidence that your sins are so perfectly taken away, that they cannot hinder you from exercising the most lively fellowship with God! Yea, consider wherein it consists to eat the flesh, and to drink the blood of Christ: remember what hath been said before, and it will excite an eager appetite in you for it, and ye will have a foretaste of it.

Dare ye not think, O weak believers, that it is for you? Hear then from Psalm 22:26, 29, that the death of Jesus is also your bread: 'The meek shall eat and be satisfied: they shall praise the LORD that seek him: your heart shall live for ever.' Not only shall 'all that be fat upon earth eat and worship: all they that go down to the dust shall bow before him: and none can keep alive his own soul.' Jesus gives you the seal and pledge of this, to strengthen, assure, and seal you; the signs are the bread and the cup of the Lord, which He Himself calls His body and blood.

**Van der Kemp, 2:88–89**

## Songs of thanks after feasting at the banquet

After such a banquet as this, thou mayest well give thanks. The Jews at their Passover did sing the hundred and thirteenth Psalm, with the five following psalms, which they called the great Hallelujah. A Christian should in everything and at all times give thanks, but at a sacrament the great Hallelujah must be sung; then God must have great thanks, then we must with our 'souls bless the Lord, and with all within us praise his holy name'.

Reader, call upon thyself, as Barak and Deborah did, 'Awake, awake, Deborah; awake, awake, utter a song; arise, Barak, and lead thy captivity captive, thou son of Abinoam' (Judges 5). 'Awake, my love; awake, my joy; utter a song.' 'A feast is made for laughter, and wine rejoiceth the heart of man.' Friend, is not this a rare feast? Where is thy cheerful face? Is not here good wine, a cup of nectar indeed, the blood of the Son of God?

What mirth, what music hast thou to this banquet of wines? Anciently it was the beginning and ending of letters, *Gaudete in domino,* rejoice in the Lord. It will be an excellent conclusion of this ordinance to rejoice in the Lord. Let thy soul 'magnify the Lord, and thy spirit rejoice in God thy Saviour' (*cf.* Luke 1:46-47).

The cup in the sacrament is called the Eucharistical cup, or 'the cup of blessing'; let it be so to thee. Let thy heart and mouth say, 'Blessed be the Lord God of Israel, who hath visited and redeemed his people' (Luke 2).

Canst thou think of that infinite love which God manifested to thy soul without David's return, 'What shall I render to the Lord for all his benefits?' His heart was so set upon thy salvation, His love was so great to thy soul, that He delighted in the very death of His Son because it tended to thy good. 'It pleased the LORD to bruise him' (Isa. 53:10). *Valde delectatus est,* Junius reads it, 'He was exceedingly delighted' in it. Surely the mind of God was infinitely set upon the recovery of lost sinners, in that — whereas other parents, whose love to their children in comparison of His to Christ is but as a drop to the ocean, follow their children to their graves with many tears, especially when they die violent deaths — He delighted exceedingly in the barbarous death of His only Son, in the bleeding of the Head, because it tended to the health and eternal welfare of the members.

Friend, 'What manner of love hath the Father loved thee with?' He gave His own Son to be apprehended, that thou mightest escape; His own Son to be condemned, that thou mightest be acquitted; His own Son to be whipped and wounded, that thou mightest be cured and healed; yea, His own Son to die a shameful cursed death, that thou mightest live a glorious blessed life for ever. 'Glory to God in the highest, peace on earth, and good will to men.'

Alas, how unworthy art thou of this inestimable mercy! Thou art by nature a child of wrath as well as others, and hadst been now wallowing in sin with the worst in the world, if free grace had not renewed thee; nay, thou hadst been roaring in hell at this hour if free grace had not reprieved thee. Thy conscience will tell thee that thou dost not deserve the bread which springeth out of the earth, and yet thou art fed with the bread which came down from heaven, with angels' food. O infinite love!

Mayest not thou well say with Mephibosheth to David, 'What is thy servant, that thou shouldest look upon such a dead dog as I am? For all my father's house were as dead men before my lord, yet didst thou set thy servant among them that did eat at thine own table.' Lord, I was a lost, dead, damned sinner before Thee, liable to the unquenchable fire, and yet Thou hast been pleased to set me among them that eat at Thine own Table, and feed on Thine own Son. Oh, what is Thy servant, that Thou shouldst take notice of such a dead dog as I am?

**Swinnock, 1:212–13**

# 12

# SELF-EXAMINATION AND WATCHFULNESS

*Wherefore let him that thinketh he standeth take heed*
*lest he fall*
(1 Corinthians 10:12).

## Thankful, humble, watchful

We should be concerned to maintain a devout frame of heart and spirit in coming from the Lord's Supper.

Spiritual frames are frequently evanescent [fleeting like a vapor]; and only in the way of holy vigilance and much prayer are they maintained, so as to give spiritual peace and consolation. The frame suitable to those who have been at the sacramental feast is one of admiration and thanksgiving and rejoicing. We should come down from the mount of communion filled with wonder at the love of God towards us, which is displayed in the ordinance; and at the grace and condescension of Christ, in taking us into covenant and communion with Himself, and in giving us the seal and earnest of the heavenly inheritance. The spirit of heartfelt humility is becoming such as have realized the presence of Christ in His ordinance, and have been with Him in the holy mount. If we have been brought near into His presence — have seen His face, and received blessing from His hands, we will be humbled under a sense of our own vileness — of our want of due preparation — of the imperfection and sin of our near approaches to God in this ordinance — the coldness of our affections, and our inadequate apprehension of the great things of God's glory and our salvation. The 'goodness of God' should 'lead us to repentance' — and, in proportion as we are made partakers of the great blessings of redemption, will we be humbled to the dust, under the sense of God's wondrous grace, and our own manifold unworthiness. Like David, when there was revealed to him God's purpose of love, and there were given to him assurances of future blessing, we should exclaim with admiration — 'Who am I, O Lord God? and what is my father's house, that Thou hast brought me hitherto? … And is this the manner of man, O Lord God' (2 Sam. 7:18-19)? Or, as Jacob, when he declared — 'I am not worthy of the least of all the mercies, and of all the truth, which Thou hast showed unto Thy servant' (Gen. 32:10).

Furthermore, a watchful frame is especially required of those who have enjoyed privilege and blessing in the sacrament. We need to watch against trusting on the sacrament, and confiding in our vows and resolutions. We should guard against the devices of Satan, and temptations to heart-wanderings, spiritual pride, and undue worldly cares — the risings of unmortified passions — and all spiritual sloth and formality in religion. A spirit of constant holy vigilance is ever needed, if we would be active and steadfast in holy obedience — if we would be preserved from leaning on our own strength, and be found looking to Christ for quickening influence, and be prepared for His coming.

**Houston, 216–18**

## Thoughtful meditations after the Supper

Be very careful to conduct yourself well after the Lord's Supper. If Satan has not been able to gain the advantage over you in the preparation for and celebration of the Lord's Supper, he will yet endeavor to get the advantage over you after the Lord's Supper.

As one must be on guard against the enemy, he must likewise take special care to conduct himself appropriately toward God, his Benefactor. We may indeed apply to this spiritual meal what God demanded of Israel upon their arrival in Canaan with its abundance: 'When thou hast eaten and art full, then thou shalt bless the LORD thy God for the good land which He hath given thee. Beware that thou forget not the LORD thy God' (Deut. 8:10-11).

Reflection consists first of all in a quiet reflection upon how we have fared at the Lord's Supper, and furthermore, how we have behaved ourselves and what God has done for us. 'And thou shalt remember all the way which the Lord thy God led thee these forty years in the wilderness' (Deut. 8:2).

Reflect upon what your condition has been.

(1) Have you been actively engaged during the time of preparation? Have you taken the time for it, or did you continually postpone it until time slipped away from you and a slight spiritual motion with a prayer or two had to do? Was there a reflection upon sin, and a wrestling to receive Christ? Was there a lively inclination and a stirring to repent, or were you in darkness, listless, and discouraged?

(2) What was your condition during the administration of the Lord's Supper? Were you sorrowful or joyful? Were you tender, or hard and insensitive — all this being intermingled with sorrow? Were you in the dark or was it light; were you moved or composed; did you exercise faith or were you full of fear? Were you filled with longing or was it barren within?

Reflect also upon the manner in which the Lord has manifested Himself to you.

(1) Were you sorrowful both when you came and when you returned, not having sensed the Lord's presence?

(2) Did you receive peace, quietness, hope, assurance, and joy? Did you sweetly cleave to the Lord, doing so while weeping, without much comfort? Or could you entrust it all to the Lord, and did you in love lean upon your Beloved? Did the Lord manifest Himself to you in a special manner with extraordinary revelations, or by granting clear and powerful assurance? Reflect upon these and similar matters. Do not deny what you have received; highly esteem the very least

thing. If the soul can thus engage itself in quiet meditation, the Lord's Supper will have a sweet aftertaste. One will perceive his failures and acknowledge the free grace of God, His goodness, and His benevolence. It will be a renewal of friendship, and be as a wedding dinner, treating Jesus to His own dainties, saying, 'Let my Beloved come into His garden, and eat His pleasant fruits' (Song 4:16). Yes, you may then receive that blessing during reflection which you missed while partaking of the Lord's Supper.

**Brakel, 2:593–94**

## Spiritual realism after the Supper

After the first sacramental communion, the apostles entered into temptation, fell asleep, and soon afterwards were guilty of greater sins. Let the young communicant be watchful against surprises. Even on the very day, the soul sometimes relaxes its vigor; as the bent bow flies back when unbound. Where the services are protracted [long], as is sometimes the case, there is a tendency to this result, from weariness of body and mind. Be exhorted to maintain seriousness and humility and quiet of soul, even though tears or rapture are denied you. What can more surely argue a shallow experience, if not a profane mind, than a speedy return to light reading, frivolous conversation, and worldly thoughts? Endeavor to preserve the sentiments which you have attained, and reflect upon the manner in which you have passed through this new and important scene of your life.

It is by no means unusual for persons to come from a first communion in deep distress. Instead of the peace and joy which they expected, they found only stupidity [spiritual dullness or sluggishness], unbelief, and vexing thoughts. Or, at best, they received no addition of faith and emotion. In such cases, they are harassed with fears, and even ready to abandon all hope. For the most part, these apprehensions are inordinate. The worst cases are those where there is no sense of dissatisfaction. The profit of the communion is not always to be measured by its comforts. The graces of the Lord's Table are sovereign and manifold. They are not always productive of joy. There may be great advancement, and true service of God, where there is no elation. The soul may be acceptable to Christ, where there are deep sorrows, or keen pangs of compunction [piercing guilt], or distressing self-condemnation. The ordinance has not been unfruitful, if it has left you low in the dust, under a persuasion of your own remaining sin, helplessness, and need of Christ. But even on the supposition that much has been wrong in the frame of your spirit, what remains for you, but to prostrate yourself anew at the feet of Jesus? Carefully review the nature of your preparation, and mark its defects. Recall your mental acts during the sacrament; inquire what has been amiss; and resolve in God's strength to avoid these evils in time to come.

Through the tender mercies of our God, the cases are numerous, in which the young communicant retires from the Table of the Lord, strengthened and encouraged. The cardinal truth of Christianity has been set before his thoughts and become incorporated with his faith. He has seen Jesus (John 12:21). His view of the infinite freedom of salvation has been made more clear. The evidences of his acceptance with God have become brighter. He is more disposed than ever before, to yield himself as a sacrifice, soul, body, and spirit, which is his reasonable service (Rom. 12:1). Where any part of this is true, you have new cause for gratitude. It is 'the LORD thy God which teacheth thee to profit' (Isa. 48:17). Now is the time, to bless Him for this grace, and to beg the continuance of it. Now is the time to set a watch against relapses, and to carry into effect the vows which you have made at the Lord's Table. Henceforth, you will look for the recurrence of this sacrament with a lively expectation, founded on experience.

**Alexander, 56–60**

## Growth does not always mean great joy

It is possible that a true Christian can sometimes be completely bereft of any spiritual joy proceeding from the Lord's Supper, and yet he receives and enjoys this Supper with genuine fruit. The reason for this is that this joy is neither an essential component of one's partaking of the Lord's Supper, nor is such joy promised in an absolute sense but rather as a conditional promise.

Another reason is that in addition to such joy, the Lord's Supper yields many other fruits. In many cases it can yield more rather than less fruit to the soul, fruits such as humility, love, zeal, and others. We will subsequently speak of these fruits.

It can therefore be concluded once more how grievous an error it is:

1) That some judge all Lord's Supper celebrations in which they did not enjoy comfort or joy as being useless and fruitless. They did attend, they confess, entirely without profit, using the argument that they attended as stocks and blocks, and were barren and dull as they partook; they also confess that they departed from the Table in that condition. It can nevertheless be that a lawful partaking of the Lord's Supper was not accompanied with such joy, and yet the soul will greatly benefit from such partaking even though she feels herself deprived at that moment from such sensible enjoyment. Though it is indeed true that all other fruitful stirrings of the heart constitute a large measure of the soul's taste and sweetness of this joy during the Lord's Supper, it does not mean that it loses its efficacy entirely, although for a season this delight is not experienced.

2) Considering that there are others who not only render a particular attendance at the Lord's Supper suspect but who occasionally view their entire spiritual state as being suspect. Such ones frequently view themselves as entirely void of grace, because they generally partake of the Lord's Supper with such a lack of feeling and joy; this is something that has already gone on for quite a length of time. This would suggest that comfort rather than sanctifying grace constitutes conversion and that the Lord's Supper yields no other fruitfulness than only this spiritual joy. We have, however, already proven and concluded the contrary.

Though it is true that consistent barrenness regarding such powerful and lively exercises cannot be reconciled with the new birth, such a conclusion is sometimes made too quickly. The fact is that both can very well co-exist. This is especially true when such barrenness is particularly defined as an absence of comfort and delight in regard to the Lord's Supper (as can be observed here and there), and not as a general lack of all holy and sanctifying motions regarding all spiritual exercises. Yes, we would even dare to add, believing it to be truly founded upon God's Word, that one who is truly born again can for a considerable period of time not only use and observe the Lord's Supper without tasting or perceiving any delight and sweetness in the same, but this can also be true for all other spiritual exercises — all the while retaining a painful sense of one's insensibility (Isa. 63:17; and 64:5, 7; Ps. 119:25; Song 5:3, 6).

**Saldenus, 27-28**

# 13

## HOLY RESOLUTIONS TO WALK WITH GOD

*And did all eat the same spiritual meat; and did all drink the
same spiritual drink: for they drank of that spiritual Rock
that followed them: and that Rock was Christ. But with many
of them God was not well pleased: for they were overthrown
in the wilderness. Now these things were our examples,
to the intent we should not lust after evil things,
as they also lusted*
(1 Corinthians 10:3-6).

### Putting the world behind us

Reflection must result in a despising and an abandoning
of the world. 'Love not the world, neither the things that
are in the world. If any man love the world, the love of the
Father is not in him. For all that is in the world, the lust of the
flesh, and the lust of the eyes, and the pride of life, is not of the
Father, but is of the world' (1 John 2:15-16). You are obliged
to abandon the world, for:

(1) This is inherent in the covenant into which you have entered and which has been sealed to you. This means that God alone is your desire, resting place, joy, delight, and the One whom I fear. The world is therefore from now on, of no significance. It is merely to be used as a means through which you traverse as a stranger in order to come to the fatherland.

(2) The world is nothing but pollution itself and lies in wickedness; you, however, are washed by the blood and Spirit of Christ. How then can you again defile yourself? The Lord has called or drawn you out of this dreadful and wicked world, as He drew Abraham out of Ur and Israel out of Egypt — how then can you return there again?

(3) Those two, God and the world, stand in direct opposition to each other; whoever loves the one hates the other, for no one can serve two masters. 'Whosoever therefore will be a friend of the world is the enemy of God' (James 4:4).

(4) The love of the world is an adulterous love, and your Bridegroom, Jesus, to whom you have been espoused, will be very jealous in response thereto. It also dishonors Him, for it is as if He could not sufficiently satisfy the soul — as if you needed something besides Him. It would then appear as if He were not sufficiently good and friendly to refresh and gladden His bride.

(5) He shall respond to such denial with more abundant comfort. The Lord shall not allow the abandonment of all that is of the world — motivated by love for Him — to go unrequited.

(6) It is nothing more than vanity. Moreover, what is the world with all its glory without Jesus?

(7) All this confusion, beloved, and all this grief, sorrow, and trouble originate nowhere else but in the world which, as your enemy, wounds you by either flattering or frightening you. Will you then seek out your own sorrow? Have you not tasted her bitterness long enough? Therefore come out of her, and let your walk henceforth be in heaven.

**Brakel, 598–99**

## Standing firm against Satan

We should come from this ordinance with a watchful fear of Satan's wiles, and a firm resolution to stand our ground against them. Whatever comfort and enlargement we have had in this ordinance, still we must remember, that we are but girding on the harness [or armour], and therefore we have no reason to boast or be secure, as though we had it put off. When we return to the world again, we must remember that we go among snares, and must provide accordingly; it is our wisdom so to do.

1. Let us therefore fear. He that travels with a rich treasure about him, is in most danger of being robbed. The ship that is richly laden, is the pirate's prize. If we come away from the Lord's Table replenished with the goodness of God's house, and the riches of His covenant, we must expect the assaults of our spiritual enemies, and not be secure.

Immediately after our Saviour was baptized, and owned by a voice from heaven, 'he was led into the wilderness to be tempted of the devil'. And immediately after He had administered the Lord's Supper to His disciples, He told them plainly, 'Satan hath desired to have you,' he has challenged you, 'that he may sift you as wheat'; and what he said to them, He says to all, 'Watch and pray, that ye enter not into temptation.'

But with particular care we must watch against the workings of spiritual pride, after a sacrament. When our Lord Jesus first instituted this ordinance, and made His disciples partakers of it, a contest immediately arose among them, which of them should be greatest. Let us dread the first risings of self-conceit, and suppress them; for, 'What have we that we have not received? And if we have received it, why then do we boast?'

2. Let us therefore fix [be firm]; and let our hearts be established with the grace here received. What we have done in this ordinance, we must go away firmly resolved to abide by all our days. I am now fixed immovably for Christ and holiness, against sin and Satan. The matter is settled, never to be called in question again: 'I will serve the Lord. Get thee behind me, Satan, thou art an offence to me. I have opened my mouth unto the Lord, and I cannot go back. I have chosen the way of truth, and therefore in Thy strength, Lord, I will stick to Thy testimonies.' Now my foot stands in an even place, well shod with the preparation of the gospel of peace. I am now like a strong man refreshed with wine, resolved to resist the devil, that he may flee from me, and never yield to him.

**Henry, *Communicant's Companion*, 247–50**

## Life-long preparation to commune with God

A great deal of care is to be used when we go to feast with the King of heaven; but that is not the greatest, much less all the care of a Christian. If God prepare a Supper, we should prepare ourselves to be fit guests (so much is resolved upon by all) the only danger is, lest we don't think this preparation looks so far back as really it doth.

A holy life is the true time for preparing our souls to be God's guests. Whatsoever care and exactness we use, and whatsoever extraordinary ornaments we put on immediately before our approaches to him; yet that a constant good behavior towards God and man is the main thing we are to look after, is the sum of what I have to say.

Holiness is to be a Christian's constant employment, and the great business of his life. It is not a quality of which we have use only at certain times, nor is it a strictness at some seasons that gets us a liberty in the rest of our lives to be loose and careless; nor a solitary retiredness now and then, that shall make an amends for all our wanderings: but it is a walking with God, a patient running of the race which He hath set us, and a daily dying unto the world, insomuch that the Apostle saith, we must be holy in all manner of conversation [or conduct] (1 Peter 1:15).

We are not to put on the Lord Jesus as we do a cloak which we throw off at our pleasure, and again cast about us when there is occasion; but as we do our inner garment which we

never go without, nor lay aside, no not when we have none in
company but ourselves.

**Patrick, *Mensa*, 148, 150–51**

## Leaving the Table to walk in love, obedience, and hope

Q. What is that suitable frame and disposition of spirit which
communicants ought to have when they rise and come from
the Lord's Table?

A. We ought to come away from this ordinance in [among
other things] a charitable frame, in a willing and obedient
frame, in a fixed and resolute frame, [and] in a longing and
heavenly frame.

Q. Wherein lies that charitable [or loving] disposition which
we ought to have when we come away from the Lord's Table?

A. 1. In bearing good will to the souls of all men, and
heartily wishing their welfare (1 Thess. 3:5, 12).

A. 2. In having a true love for all the members of Christ's
mystical body and in bearing with them, though in various
things they differ from us.

A. 3. In a readiness to relieve the poor and indigent
[destitute] according to our ability (Gal. 6:10).

A. 4. In a disposition to forgive those who have been
injurious to us. And surely all who have been sharers of God's
mercy and grace in the sacrament will come away from it
with such a charitable disposition.

Q. What is that willing and obedient frame which communicants
ought to have when they come from the Lord's Table?

A. It lies in these things:

1. In a grateful sense of the many ties and obligations we are under to serve Him.

2. In making it our great scope and design to approve ourselves to God in all things.

3. In making it our study to know God's mind and will, and what it is that is most acceptable and pleasing to Him.

4. In having a universal respect to all God's commands, and a readiness of mind for every good work.

5. In being active and zealous for the glory of God and the interest of His kingdom among men.

Q. What is that fixed and resolute frame which they ought to have?

A. It is the soul's deliberate and steadfast resolution to adhere to Christ, His ways, and His interest, in the midst of trials and difficulties. We must now be at a point in this matter where we are fully determined, by the grace of God, to look and to go forward in our Christian course, and that no solicitation or temptation shall move us either to look back or to draw back, but that with purpose of heart we will cleave unto the Lord (Ps. 119:30-31, 115; Acts 11:23).

Q. What is the longing and heavenly frame which we ought to have when we come from the Lord's Table?

A. It consists in these things:

1. In a firm belief in Christ's second coming, and in the life everlasting.

2. In a lively meditation upon Christ's coming and future glory.

3. In an earnest looking for that blessed hope, and a joyful expectation of the glory to be revealed (Titus 2:13; Rom. 5:2).

4. In a constant watching and preparing for the coming of the Bridegroom (Luke 12:36-37).

**Willison,** *Sacramental Catechism,* **265, 270–72**

## United to Christ, imitating Christ

The purpose of your partaking of the Lord's Supper is to set before your eyes the most intimate union that exists between you and the Lord Jesus Christ, a union that has been cemented by the Holy Spirit. When someone eats, not only is there a close interaction between the food that is being eaten and the one eating it, but that same food will partially be transformed into his own substance. Consider therefore what it means for you to eat the body of the Lord Jesus and to drink His blood so that you would trust all the more in Him with whom such a very intimate union has been established.

There is also an intimate relationship between husband and wife. How can we actually express what that union consists of? And yet how can that compare to the union we may have with Christ when we eat His flesh and drink His blood? The husband neither eats his wife, nor the wife her husband. The body and blood of the one is not spiritual food and drink for the other, as is this spiritual union with Christ. Yes, however intimate spouses may be with one another, they nevertheless have each their own soul. The soul of the husband is not the soul of the wife, and the wife has a soul that is not the husband's. However, our union with Christ is quite another and a far superior matter. By eating His flesh and drinking His blood, we become of one spirit with Him (1 Cor. 6:17). His Spirit is our spirit, and our spirit is His. 'For by one Spirit are we all baptized into one body.' How would we not believe all the more firmly in what the proper use of the Lord's Supper teaches us, namely, that He has become one with us in such a fashion as we ourselves experience it?

Is it your desire to be more obedient to God? Consider then in the Lord's Supper who the person is with whom you are so intimately united. Consider how pure He is and not tarnished by any form of disobedience. How it behooves you therefore to resist as little as possible the will of Him with whom you are so intimately united! When you truly meditate upon this, can you then possibly love what He hates and hate what He so tenderly loves? This would truly be as if you desired to oppose yourself, since you are flesh of His flesh and bone of His bones. To be disobedient toward God, while desiring simultaneously to be the beneficiary of the perfect obedience of Christ, is nothing less than desiring to combine light and darkness, God and Satan, and virtue and sin.

If, by way of the Lord's Supper, you also desire to grow in patience, so that you will neither murmur nor grieve when God afflicts you, then compare your suffering with the breaking, crucifixion, and killing of the body of Christ which you may eat in the Lord's Supper. Consider, then, how insignificant your affliction is when compared with His. Where are your scourgings? Where are your crowns of thorns? Where are your drops of blood? Where has God been opposed to you as a provoked judge? When have you experienced hell in your soul? Compare your suffering once with all this, and consider whether your cross is not merely one made of straw and feathers in comparison with His iron and accursed cross? And what else would we not be able to add if we were inclined to enlarge upon this?

And observe also in the Lord's Supper the willingness of Christ in all His sufferings and how readily and unreservedly He surrendered Himself. He as willingly surrendered His body and blood, whereof the bread and wine are seals, as these are given to you by the minister. He was led as a lamb to the slaughter, and as a sheep before her shearers is dumb, so He opened not His mouth (Isa. 53:7). Instead, 'He humbled himself, and became obedient unto death, even the death of the cross' (Phil. 2:8). 'Behold,' so He spoke, 'I delight to do Thy will, O my God' (Ps. 40:8). There is no part in His suffering to which He was compelled to submit, even as the minister is not compelled to distribute the bread at the Lord's Supper. When considering this, should you then, as it were, have to be dragged by your hair in order to follow Him when often you have to endure no more than a sour face or a sharp word for the sake of His truth, or even when you have to endure a fever, an illness, or whatever else might be?

**Saldenus, 66-69**

## The pleasures of fellowship with God

Reflection consists in a continual looking unto and having fellowship with the Lord. Therefore set the Lord continually before you and live in a continual dialogue with Him — at one time pray, then ask for counsel, then express your dependence upon Him, then wait upon Him, then reverently worship Him, then rest in Him, then thank Him, and then again, offer yourself to His service. Acquaint yourself thus with Him.

All salvation, comfort, delight, holiness, and felicity for the soul is to be found in having fellowship with God. Such a soul perceives the righteousness of God as being only light, glorious, and pure — she loves it and rejoices herself in it, doing so all the more, since this righteousness is not against her unto condemnation, but the Surety having merited this, it is to her advantage. The soul also perceives the goodness and all-sufficiency of God, and in enjoying their efficacy, she not only is unable to find any desirability in creatures apart from God, but apart from God there is nothing which she desires, since the soul finds everything in God. The soul also perceives the holiness of God. Since she is unable to endure its luster [brightness], she covers her countenance and perceives in this luster her own sinfulness; and for shame, she shrivels away, so to speak, and becomes as nothing.

The soul also perceives the love of God, and being irradiated by this love, she delights herself in a most wondrous way, reciprocal love being ignited within her. She perceives the will of God as being uppermost and sovereign over all things. Thus, she loses her own will in whatever suffering comes her way and in whatever duties are before her. She wishes it to be thus because it is the Lord's will. The soul perceives the majesty and glory of God, in comparison with which all creatures lose their majesty and glory and she bows herself deeply before her majestic God, worships Him with deep reverence and gives honor and glory to Him. She perceives the omnipotence of God, both within Himself and as it is operative toward His creatures. Then the power of the creature, which manifests itself either for or against her will, disappears. She sees the wisdom of God as revealing itself in all His works — both in nature as well as in grace. Thus, the wisdom of all creatures melts away and she is quiet and well-satisfied with the only wise government of God. The soul also perceives the veracity and faithfulness of God. She is acquainted with the promises, believes them, and is so confident as far as the certainty of these promises is concerned, that it is as if they were already fulfilled.

All this engenders a thoughtful and steadfast spiritual frame, quiet submission in whatever circumstances the soul encounters, a fearless courage in the performance of her duty, and a delighting herself in the task she has done for the Lord, leaving the outcome with resignation to the Lord's direction. Such a life is truly a joyful life, and pure holiness issues forth from this. She acknowledges any virtue which is not practiced by having God in Christ in view, as a vice. Such fellowship with God is heaven itself: 'and so shall we ever be with the Lord. Wherefore comfort one another with these words' (1 Thess. 4:17-18). David says of this: 'In Thy presence is fulness of joy; at Thy right hand there are pleasures for evermore' (Ps. 16:11).

Behold, such is the eminent felicity of fellowship with God.
**Brakel, 596–97**

# 14

# PRAYERS OF THANKSGIVING

*The L*ORD *is my strength and song, and is become my*
*salvation. The voice of rejoicing and salvation*
*is in the tabernacles of the righteous:*
*the right hand of the L*ORD *doeth valiantly*
(Psalm 118:14-15).

## God exalted, me abased

O most Holy, Holy, Holy, Lord God Almighty; heaven and earth are full of the glory of Thy majesty. Glory be unto Thee, O God most high, Thou great Creator and Possessor of heaven and earth; Thou Preserver of all things, Thou spring of eternal mercy; who hast so loved mankind, that Thou hast opened Thy bosom and sent Thy dear Son to convey Thy charity to us. All laud and praise and thanksgiving be to Thee, O Father of mercies, who hast now made me taste how gracious and good Thou art.

And glory be to the Son of God, who took on Him the form of a servant; who died for us upon the cross; who purged away our sins by His blood; who hath left us so many remembrances of His love; and given us His body and blood to preserve our souls and bodies to eternal life: who lives for ever to make intercession for us; and hath promised to come again and take us up unto himself.

And blessed Holy Spirit, the mighty power of God; the Author of all good thoughts; the Inspirer of all heavenly desires; the light and comfort of our minds; the Purifier of our hearts; the Guide and strength of our life; who hath given us the earnest of the eternal inheritance.

I have now tasted of the abundance of Thy grace and dearest love: the favour of which, O that it may remain fresh for ever in my heart: that I may live for ever in Thy love, and be ready to die for Thy love: that I may delight to do Thy will, O God, and be content to suffer it, as the blessed Jesus did. And, O that I may never forget to feed on Him daily by faith and love, till He indeed live in me, and I in Him; and all the powers of my soul and body be employed by His counsels, and not my own. O that my life may be an exact imitation of Him, and express His perfections, and show forth His virtues, and declare to all how much I love Him. Especially endue me with great humility and modesty of spirit; that I may live in a constant remembrance of Thee my Creator: and considering that Thou art the Author of every good gift, may never be puffed up, nor do anything through strife and vainglory; but in lowliness of mind esteem others better than myself (Phil.

2:3-5). O that the same mind may be in me, which was also in Christ Jesus: who being in the form of God, made Himself of no reputation, and took upon Him the form of a servant; and humbling Himself became obedient unto death, even the death of the cross.

**Patrick, *The Christian Sacrifice*, 149–52**

## Sin crucified, Christ alive in me

O Lord, my God and my Father in Jesus Christ, I can never sufficiently admire the condescension of Thy grace to me; what is man that Thou dost thus magnify him, and the son of man that Thou thus visitest him! Who am I? And what is my house, that Thou has brought me hitherto; hast brought me into the banqueting-house, and Thy banner over me hath been love? I have reason to say, that a day in Thy courts, an hour at Thy Table, is better, far better, than a thousand days, than ten thousand hours elsewhere; it is good for me to draw near to God: blessed be God for the privileges of His house, and those comforts with which He makes His people joyful in His house of prayer.

But I have reason to blush and be ashamed of myself that I have not been more affected with the great things which have been set before me, and offered to me at the Lord's Table. O what a vain, foolish, and trifling heart have I! When I would do good, even evil is present with me. Good Lord, be merciful to me, and pardon the iniquity of my holy things, and let not my many defects in my attendance upon Thee be laid to my charge, or hinder my profiting by the ordinance.

I have now been commemorating the death of Christ; Lord, grant that by the power of that, sin may be crucified in me, the world crucified to me, and I to the world: and enable me so to bear about with me continually the dying of the Lord Jesus, as that the life also of Jesus may be manifested in my mortal body.

All my outward affairs I submit to the disposal of Thy wise and gracious providence; Lord, save my soul, and then as to other things do as Thou pleasest with me; only make all providences work together for my spiritual and eternal advantage. Let all things be pure to me, and give me to taste covenant love, in common mercies; and by Thy grace let me be taught, both how to want [lack], and how to abound, how to enjoy prosperity, and how to bear adversity as becomes a Christian: and at all times let Thy grace be sufficient for me, and mighty in me, to work in me both to will and to do that which is good of Thine own good pleasure.

And that in everything I may do my duty, and stand complete in it, let my heart be enlarged in love to Jesus Christ, and affected with the height and depth, the length and breadth of that love of His to me, which passeth all conception and expression.

And as an evidence of that love, let my mouth be filled with His praises. Worthy is the Lamb that was slain to receive blessing, and honour, and glory and power; for He was slain, and hath redeemed a chosen remnant unto God by His blood, and made them to Him kings and priests. Bless the Lord, O my soul, and let all that is within me bless His holy name, who forgiveth all mine iniquities, and healeth all my diseases; who redeemeth my life from destruction, and crowneth me with Thy loving-kindness and tender mercy; who has begun a good work, and will perform it unto the day of Christ. As long as I live will I bless the Lord; I will praise my God while I have any being; and when I have no being upon earth, I hope to have a being in heaven to be doing it better. O let me be borne up in everlasting arms, and carried from strength to strength, till I appear before God in Zion, for Jesus' sake, who died for me, and rose again, in whom I desire to be found living and dying. Now to God the Father, Son, and Spirit be ascribed kingdom, power and glory, henceforth and for ever. Amen.

**Henry,** *Method for Prayer*, **245–48**

## Breathings of love for Christ

Do I not love Thee, O my Saviour? I humbly trust I can say, 'Thou knowest all things, thou knowest that I love Thee.' Either I am a stranger to my own heart, and ignorant after what objects it breathes and aspires, or I unfeignedly [sincerely], I prevailingly love Thee. Art Thou the darling of Thine almighty Father, His chief delight? And art Thou not mine? Does not my soul follow hard after Thee; prefer Thy friendship to that of the whole world; esteem all those marks and traces of Thine image, which prove my relation to Thee, and interest in Thee, more than the peculiar treasure of kings? Does it not ardently desire to be better acquainted with Thee, according to the discoveries that are made of Thee in the gospel? Would not all the pleasures and entertainments of life be insipid, and even tiresome, without Thee? To be with Thee, would not my soul willingly quit the body, even this moment, didst Thou call her, and she were assured that her separation from all things here below would be followed with a nearer union with Thee?

I love Thee, O Jesus; but not as I would, not as I ought to love Thee! When I think of Thy personal excellencies, Thy condescension, Thy sufferings, Thy death and the glorious fruits of them; I am not able to conceive, much less describe the love I owe Thee. I can only say in general, that my love should have no other bounds than the capacity of my heart; I should love Thee as much as I can love Thee, and thus it is I would love Thee. O let Thy love kindle mine; let it mount into a flame; let this flame consume every visionary [or imaginary] idol that usurps any part of the honour due to my Saviour; let it enliven every power, direct and consecrate every thought, every affection, every design; let me, and all I possess, be a sacrifice of love; to Thee I devote it all, through whom all things are mine, and who art more than all other things can possibly be to me!

What abundant reason, O most blessed Saviour, have I to rejoice and be glad in Thee! In Thee I have determined to rejoice always; in the contemplation of Thy person, Thy gospel, Thy virtues, Thy conquests, and Thy glory, and even in Thy cross; in all the great things Thou hast done for us, and we already enjoy; and in the much greater Thou hast promised, and we yet further wait for. I will heighten the common pleasures of this life by my joy in Thee; and, by rejoicing in Thee under all the evils and troubles of it, will learn to forget or make light of them all, and to weep as if I wept not. Thou art my sanctuary and my hope. Here I take refuge when pursued by my griefs, and doubts and fears; even in Thee, and the several ways I have of conversing with Thee. O Jesus, Thou givest light to those that are in darkness, strength to the weak, rest to the weary, and comfort to the distressed! O my Saviour, as nothing is wanting in the way of assistance and encouragement on Thy part, I hope less shall be wanting on mine than hath hitherto been, in returns of praise, and service, and obedience for the unsearchable riches of Thy goodness!

**Grove, 148–51**

## Glory be to Thee, My Saviour

Glory be to Thee, O Lord, our God, that in our extreme need of a Redeemer, Thou hast made such gracious provision for our souls; that Thou hast sent Thy Son to die for our sins, and to save us, after we had destroyed ourselves. Blessed be Thy name, that He who offered Himself upon the cross for us, is pleased to offer Himself at His Table to us; there have I been tasting the fruits of His love, and receiving my share among the redeemed of the Lord. O blessed be God for so great a mercy!

I bless Thee, my God, for the mercies of a Saviour; without which all other mercies would be of no avail, would do me no good. I bless Thee, that Thou hast not withheld Thy Son, Thine only Son from us; but hast given Him to be the propitiation for our sins, and the life and food of our souls.

I sat down under His shadow, and His fruit was sweet to my taste, I have been entertained at the Table of the Lord; and there His banner over me was love. It was love that gave me the Saviour whom I have been receiving; and the opportunity to rest and feast my soul upon Him.

Return to thy rest, O my soul, for the Lord has dealt bountifully with thee. Thy life is given thee at His hands, who forgiveth all thy sins, and healeth all thy diseases; and not only redeems thee from destruction, but crowns thee with loving-kindness and tender mercies; and satisfies thy mouth with good things, even with pardon and peace, yea, with the riches of His grace, and the pledges of His glory.

Eternal thanks and praise be unto Thee, O blessed God, my Saviour, for all Thy glorious achievements, in laying the sure foundation for our hope, and everlasting consolation.

**Blair, 116–17**

## Straining to glorify the infinite God

O God! Thy love in Christ Jesus deserves to be praised, admired, and magnified! There is all that in it, which can engage a soul to break forth into praises, and hallelujahs! There is beauty, wisdom, condescension, mercy, liberality, sweetness, power, greatness, majesty in it, and all these in the highest degree; which would force even a dumb [mute] man to speak of Thy glory!

I adore Thee, O holy, blessed, and glorious Trinity, for that infinite care of my immortal soul, which I see in all Thy proceedings, and transactions; and particularly, in the cross of my dearest Redeemer! Here Thou seemest to empty all Thy stores, and pourest out Thy graces abundantly upon the heads and hearts of Thy servants.

O charming Son of God! I alone am not able sufficiently to praise Thee; and therefore I wish that every drop of the ocean, every grain of sand, every leaf of the trees of the field, and every sprig of herbs, and all the creatures that ever were, or are, or shall be, might be turned into seraphic tongues, to praise Thee!

O Jesus! When I behold Thy wonderful love, how it hath bowed, how it hath stooped to so mean [or lowly] a creature as I am, the thoughts of it force my soul into the humblest and deepest prostrations.

Oh, how blind are poor mortals, who are so very fond of honours, riches, curious [or elegant] palaces, gardens, pleasures, music, rarities, colours, herbs, flowers, stones, and minerals. Great Conqueror of my soul! Thou art more honourable, more amiable, more sweet, more pleasant, more agreeable, more delicious, more harmonious to my soul than all these! Thy excellency cannot, by searching, be found out!

O Lamb of God! With the four and twenty elders, I fall down before Thy throne, and cry, 'Blessing, and praise, and honour, and wisdom be unto the Lamb forever and ever; for Thou wast slain, and hast redeemed us to God, by Thy blood, out of every kindred, and tongue, and people and nation!'

O God of glory! I beseech Thee remove from me all those things which would hinder me from glorifying Thee!

**Horneck, 618–20**

# SELECTED BIBLIOGRAPHY OF CITED WORKS

Alexander, James W. *Plain Words to a Young Communicant.* New York: Anson D. F. Randolph, 1858.

Bennett, Arthur, ed. *The Valley of Vision: A Collection of Puritan Prayers and Devotions.* Edinburgh: Banner of Truth, 2002.

Bickersteth, Edward. *A Treatise on the Lord's Supper.* New York: Thomas N. Stanford, 1857.

Blair, Hugh. *A Companion to the Altar; Shewing the Nature and Necessity of a Sacramental Preparation, In order to our worthy receiving the Holy Communion.* London: Weed and Rider, for Scatcherd and Letterman, 1820.

Brakel, Wilhelmus à. 'The Lord's Supper' and 'The Practice of the Lord's Supper Consisting in Preparation, Celebration, and Reflection.' In *The Christian's Reasonable Service,* trans. Bartel Elshout, ed. Joel R. Beeke, 2:525–600. Grand Rapids: Reformation Heritage Books, 1999.

Bruce, Robert. *Robert Bruce's Sermons on the Sacrament,* ed. John Laidlaw. Edinburgh: Oliphant, Anderson and Ferrier, 1901.

Calamy, Edmund. 'The Lord's Supper Is a Federal Ordinance.' In *The Puritans on the Lord's Supper,* ed. Don Kistler. Morgan, Pa.: Soli Deo Gloria, 1997.

Calvin, John. *Treatises on the Sacraments,* trans. Henry Beveridge. Reprint, Ross-shire, Great Britain: Christian Focus, 2002.

Charnock, Stephen. Discourses on 'The Lord's Supper.' In *The Works of Stephen Charnock,* 4:392–493. 1865. Reprint, Edinburgh: Banner of Truth, 1985.

— 'A Discourse upon the Goodness of God.' In *The Complete Works of Stephen Charnock,* 2:275–399. Edinburgh: James Nichol, 1864; reprint, Edinburgh: Banner of Truth, 2010.

Day, Richard. *A Booke of Christian Prayers.* 1578. Facsimile Reprint, Amsterdam: Theatrum Orbis Terrarum, 1977.

Dod, John, and R[obert] Cleaver. *Ten Sermons, Tending chiefly to the fitting of men for the worthy receiuing of the Lord's Svpper.* London: by T. C. and R. C. for William Sheffard, 1628.

Doolittle, Thomas. *A Treatise Concerning the Lord's Supper,* ed. Don Kistler. Morgan, Pa.: Soli Deo Gloria, 1998.

Downame, John. *A Treatise Tending to direct the weak Christian, How he may rightly celebrate the Sacrament of the Lord's Supper.* London: Philemon Stephens, 1645.

Earle, Jabez. *Sacramental Exercises.* 4th ed. London: Richard Hett, 1742.

Edwards, Jonathan. *Sermons on the Lord's Supper,* ed. Don Kistler. Orlando: Northampton Press, 2007.

Fenner, William. 'The Punishment of Unworthy Communicants at the Table of the Lord,' and 'The Dutie of Communicants: Or, Examination required of every

Communicant.' In *The Works of W. Fenner,* 83–117. [London]: by E. Tyler for I. Stafford, 1657.

Flavel, John. 'An Exposition of the Assembly's Catechism.' In *The Works of John Flavel,* 6:138–317. 1820. Reprint, Edinburgh: Banner of Truth, 1997.

— 'The Fountain of Life,' sermon 21, on 1 Corinthians 11:23–25. In *The Works of John Flavel,* 1:259–70. 1820. Reprint, Edinburgh: Banner of Truth, 1997.

— 'Sacramental Meditations' and 'A Familiar Conference between a Minister and a Doubting Christian, Concerning the Sacrament of the Lord's Supper.' In *The Works of John Flavel,* 6:378–469. 1820. Reprint, Edinburgh: Banner of Truth, 1997.

Fleetwood, W. *The Reasonable Communicant: Or, An Explanation of the Doctrine of the Sacrament of the Lord's Supper.* London: John Francis and Charles Rivington, 1784.

Grove, Henry. *A Discourse Concerning the Nature and Design of the Lord's Supper.* Salem: by Joshua Cushing, for Cushing and Appleton, 1812.

Haweis, Thomas. *The Communicant's Spiritual Companion; Or, An Evangelical Preparation for the Lord's Supper.* New Haven: Oliver Steele, 1811.

Henry, Matthew. *The Communicant's Companion; Or, Instructions for the Right Receiving of the Lord's Supper.* Philadelphia: Presbyterian Board of Publication, 1825.

— *A Method for Prayer,* ed. J. Ligon Duncan III. Greenville, S.C.: Reformed Academic Press, 1994.

Horneck, Anthony. *The Crucified Jesus: Or, A Full Account of the Nature, End, Design, and Benefits of the Sacrament of the Lord's Supper*. 7th ed. London: A. Bettesworth, 1728.

Houston, Thomas. *The Lord's Supper: Its Nature, Ends, and Obligations; and Mode of Administration*. Edinburgh: James Gemmell, 1878.

Kevan, E. F. *The Lord's Supper*. Welwyn, England: Evangelical Press, 1985.

Luckey, Samuel. *The Lord's Supper*. New York: Carlton and Porter, 1859.

Manton, Thomas. 'Several Sermons Preached on Public Occasions.' In *The Complete Works of Thomas Manton*, 15:297–499. London: James Nisbet, 1873.

Molyneux, Capel. *The Lord's Supper*. London: James Nisbet, 1850.

Owen, John. 'Sacramental Discourses.' In *The Works of John Owen*, 9:517–622. 1850–1853. Reprint, Edinburgh: Banner of Truth, 1990.

Oxenden, Ashton. *The Earnest Communicant*. Grand Rapids: Reformation Heritage Books, 2009.

Patrick, Simon. *The Christian Sacrifice. A Treatise Shewing the Necessity, End and Manner of Receiving the Holy Communion*. 8th ed. London: L. Meredith, 1687.

— *Mensa Mystica; Or A Discourse Concerning the Sacrament of the Lord's Supper*. 4th ed. London: R. W. for Francis Tyton, 1676.

Pemble, William. *An Introdvction to the Worthy Receiving the Sacrament of the Lord's Supper*. London: H. L. for Iames Boler, 1628.

Pierce, Samuel Eyles. *A Companion for the Lord's Table*. London: Samuel Pierce, 1809.

Reynolds, Edward. 'Meditations on the Holy Sacrament of the

Lord's Last Supper.' In *The Whole Works of the Right Rev. Edward Reynolds*, 3:I-163. 1826. Reprint, Morgan, Pa.: Soli Deo Gloria, 1999.

Roberts, Francis. *A Communicant Instructed: Or, Practical Directions for Worthy Receiving of the Lord's-Supper.* London: by T. R. and E. M. for George Calvert, 1651.

Saldenus, Guilelmus, 'Efficacy of the Lord's Supper to the Comfort and Sanctification of God's Children.' In *In Remembrance of Him: Profiting from the Lord's Supper,* trans. Bartel Elshout; ed. James A. De Jong, 15-82. Grand Rapids: Reformation Heritage Books, 2012.

Sibbes, Richard. 'The Right Receiving.' In *Works of Richard Sibbes,* ed. Alexander B. Grosart, 4:59–74. 1862–1864. Reprint, Edinburgh: Banner of Truth, 2001.

Swinnock, George. 'The Christian Man's Calling,' part 1, chapters 18–20. In *The Works of George Swinnock,* 1:172–222. 1868. Reprint, Edinburgh: Banner of Truth, 1992.

Van der Kemp, Johannes. *The Christian Entirely the Property of Christ, in Life and Death, Exhibited in Fifty-three Sermons on the Heidelberg Catechism,* trans. John M. Harlingen. Vol. 2. 1810. Reprint, Grand Rapids: Reformation Heritage Books, 1997.

Vincent, Nathanael. *The True Touchstone Which shews both Grace and Nature. Or, A Discourse concerning Self-Examination, by which both Saints and Sinners may come to know themselves. Whereunto Are added sundry Meditations relating to the Lord's Supper.* London: J. Richard for Tho. Parkhurst, 1681.

Vines, Richard. *A Treatise of the Institution, Right Administration, and Receiving of the Sacrament of the*

*Lord's-Supper*. London: A. M. for Thomas Underhill, 1657.

Wadsworth, Thomas. 'How may it appear to be every Christian's indispensable duty to partake of the Lord's Supper?' In *Puritan Sermons, 1659–1689,* 2:128–44. Wheaton, Ill.: Richard Owen Roberts, 1981.

Willison, John. *A Sacramental Catechism, or A Familiar Instructor for Young Communicants,* ed. Don Kistler. Morgan, Pa.: Soli Deo Gloria, 2000.

— *Sacramental Meditations and Advices*. Edinburgh: Thomas Lumisden, 1747.

Wisse, Gerard. 'May I Partake of the Lord's Supper?' In *Christ's Ministry in the Christian: The Administration of His Offices in the Believer,* trans. Bartel Elshout and William Van Voorst, 97-123. Sioux Center, Iowa.: Netherlands Reformed Book and Publishing, 1993.

Witsius, Herman. 'Of the Lord's Supper.' In *The Economy of the Covenants between God and Man,* trans. William Crookshank, 2:444–64. 1822. Reprint, Phillipsburg, N.J.: Presbyterian and Reformed Publishing, 1990.